The Six Habits
of Highly Effective
Sales Engineers

The Six Habits of Highly Effective Sales Engineers

Chris White

The Six Habits of Highly Effective Sales Engineers

ISBN-13: 978-0-578-52190-9
Kindle/PDF: 978-0-578-52190-9

Cover design by Luisito C. Pangilinan

DemoDoctor LLC DBA Tech Sales Advisors
Leesburg, VA 20176
USA

www.TechSalesAdvisors.com

If you're a Sales Engineer, *The Six Habits of Sales Engineers* is a must read. It is comprehensive, covering pre-demo discovery, demonstration planning, delivering technical demos, and as Chris calls it the 'demo aftermath.' Yet, it is simple to remember and apply as it is sectioned into Partner, Probe, Prepare, Practice, Perform, and Perfect. Since Chris has spent his career as a Sales Engineer, the book is real world. Chris has lived in the trenches, so he tells it like it is, with relatable stories about working with counterparts, prospects, and customers. The principles in this book will enable any Sales Engineer, new to the field or tenured, to deliver winning demonstrations.

—Brian Geery
Author, *How to Demonstrate Software So People Buy It*

With relatively little content available to help sales engineers perfect their craft, *The Six Habits* is a welcome and much needed addition to the SE toolkit. Chris goes beneath the surface level to examine some of the underlying challenges that place a drag on an SE's effectiveness, and offers actionable tactics to address them.

—Rob Falcone
Author, Just F*ing Demo!

Creative engineers, product designers, pioneering scientists and entrepreneurial high-tech mavericks all face a difficult challenge: *How do I get the world to not only grasp my newfangled idea, but embrace it?* When it comes to persuading others to buy in, the mastery and brilliance that brought the idea into being is the very thing that gets in the way. With just the right mix of art and science, Chris White brings a rare blend of natural talents and boatloads of experience to reverse engineer, reveal, and playfully communicate the inner works of a mysterious process that stumps the best of us.

—Anthony Spadafore
Founder, Pathfinders | Career Design Consulting

Every sales engineer should read this book! These behaviors don't come naturally to the technically minded, but Chris does a great job of laying out the essentials. I guarantee you will close more deals if you make this required reading for your technical team.

—Craig A.
Senior Account Executive
Fortune 100 Software Company

As a management consultant, I am often subjected to demos by product companies. An over-keen 'techie' tries to show us all the bells and whistles of the product he/she is proud of. The looks of boredom and bemusement on the faces of the attendees do not deter the demonstrator from the task. In fact, there seems to be no communication whatsoever between demonstrator and demonstratee! By the end the poor product salesman has no idea if the attendees are more likely to buy, because no one asked them what questions they wanted to have answered in the first place.

I had the privilege to see Chris' first workshop presenting his six principles. I just wished all the sales engineers (SE) I had been subjected to in the past had been introduced to these simple and practical principles. I recently attended a demo and was surprised when the SE asked me beforehand what I wanted to get out of the demo. During the demo he proceeded to meet my stated needs in a simple but engaging manner. By the end the salesman felt confident a sale was highly likely. When I congratulated the SE, he told me he had learned from the best – Chris White!

Chris Collins
Chairman, i-Realise Ltd

The Six Habits is fantastic. I just wish this was available to me at age 24 when I started in this industry.

—Jim D.
Director Solution Architect
Fortune 100 Software Company

About the Author

Chris White, is a recognized expert in software technical presales. He has given and observed literally hundreds, if not thousands of enterprise software demonstrations during a career that has spanned nearly three decades. He is known for his ability to deliver insightful, engaging, and highly compelling sales demos. His style and approach are both appreciated by customers and esteemed by colleagues.

The Six Habits emerged as a result of a need to develop training for a team of presales consultants that he was responsible for years ago. Through personal trial and error, observing some of the best sales engineers in the business, and experiencing both victory and defeat, Chris packaged his methods and approach into a framework of teachable, learnable, repeatable best practices, tips and techniques. Now, after years of presenting, teaching, curating and refining his message, and coaching countless others to achieve extraordinary success, he unveils this wealth of knowledge to the industry in the form of *The Six Habits of Highly Effective Sales Engineers*.

After decades of service in the field as a sales engineer, sales engineer leader, account executive, and sales enablement leader, Mr. White now runs a sales training organization called Tech Sales Advisors (www.techsalesadvisors.com), dedicated to the training and enablement of technology sales teams across the globe.

Dedication

This book is dedicated to my father, Bernard F. White, Jr, who passed on 7 December 2017, Pearl Harbor Day.

"Work hard and play hard, Chris!"

Thanks Dad. I think you'd be proud.

To my four great kids, Bradley, Greg, Anna, and Holly, and my infinitely inquisitive stepdaughter Alexandra.

I hope this inspires all of you to think big and reach for the stars.

To my wife Chawn, who has supported me from day one, through long days, late nights, and grumpy mornings.

Thanks for everything dear. You're the best. I love you.

—Chris White

Table of Contents

List of Figures and Tables

Foreword

Simply put, the Six Habits work. I have a unique perspective as I first had the opportunity to observe and experience them in action as a customer, and I have since learned and implemented them as a sales engineer.

In my former role, as VP of Software Engineering at a data and analytics company, I oversaw a strategic IT transformation project. I often dreaded interaction with software vendors – another tool, another vendor, another "best of breed, save the world with my solution" pitch. I quite literally avoided my phone in fear of being "vendorized".

Immediately Chris was different. He came totally prepared, clearly having done his homework. He asked meaningful questions. We discussed my problems and objectives first, and then how the technology could support it—as opposed to the reverse. He was incredibly effective and efficient with my time and focused on business value and project success, weeding out unnecessary noise. He treated the engagement as a partnership, and together we secured the budget for the project from the CIO, as a team.

The project itself was, in essence, a two-year internal sales engagement that included running dozens of workshops with technology teams across a vast organization. We had to prove the business value of transformation and how the newly implemented process and technology were going to drive business value. The success of the project depended on getting buy in from technical principals from across the company - i.e., getting the technical win. In hindsight, I recognize that it was the implementation and practice of the six habits that, in part, made the project so successful.

About two years ago I decided to make a career change and joined a technology company as a sales engineer. Even though I had been in technology for decades, taught computer courses for years, and ran dozens of workshops, the role of SE was new to me. I was also smart enough to know that Chris is *The Expert* in sales engineering, and I needed his help. As such, I took the "Six Habits of Effective Sales Engineers" online course during the transition. It dramatically accelerated the learning curve and enabled me to become immediately and highly effective in the role.

What makes The Six Habits so unique is that it is such a complete and comprehensive list of tips, techniques and best practices that has been assembled and packaged in such a tight and digestible manner. Anyone in software sales, whether that's direct sales, sales management or sales engineering, will benefit from this book. And for those of you considering the move or in transition, you need this book.

Today, I love my role as an SE. I enjoy the interaction of people and technology. I thrive on the opportunity to help customers reach their goals. I keep the Six Habits at the ready and refer to them regularly, especially before large engagements. After all, I don't want to just be a sales engineer, I want to be a great sales engineer.

—**Stephen Brown**
Sr. Principal Solutions Architect

Preface

Allow me to begin by sharing a few short stories that eventually led to the creation of the content you're about to read. The first happened shortly after I accepted my first job as a sales engineer (SE) – or "application engineer" (AE) as we were called at the time. I was at a cocktail party when I struck up a conversation with a gentleman whom I had not met before and the conversation, as it is so often inclined to do, turned to work. At one point he asks, "So what do you do for a living?"

Before I share with you my response to this innocent question, let me offer some context. I had been an IT professional for about 15 years before I made the jump to technical presales. I graduated from college in 1991 with a degree in Computer Information Systems (James Madison University in Virginia. Go Dukes!) I got my first job as a software engineer with Freddie Mac, a company at the time that very few people had ever heard of, but now one that most are familiar with for many of the wrong reasons.

After three years there, I made the leap to IT consulting and for 10 years held various consulting positions and roles. I worked numerous engagements as a consultant, but the foundation of my work was architecture and data – enterprise architecture, information architecture, data warehousing, business intelligence, etc. I share this context with you to say that, when I made the leap to technical presales, I was a "technology guy". In fact, I was considered an expert in my field. And I took pride in that. My education was in technology, NOT sales and marketing. My experience was in technical roles. I had never received any formal sales training. Never considered myself a sales person. Never thought I'd be in sales. It was "beneath me" —or so I thought at the time.

Incidentally, you might be asking yourself "Why then did you make the move to technical presales, Chris?" It's a valid question, and one that I will address briefly. I hit a point in my consulting career where

I found myself getting bored very quickly with each new consulting engagement I was assigned to. I'd be assigned to a new project. "Figure things out." Make some recommendations or implement a strategy, and then I'd be ready and eager to move onto a new project. To be honest, I thought there was something wrong with me because most of my colleagues were looking for 2- to 3-year projects to work on. Yet, I was typically looking to get out after 3-6 months.

I went through a professional career coaching program and discovered that there was nothing wrong with me at all; I just had some unique talents, and some very strong tendencies that needed an outlet. I needed a role that would provide for short bursts of engagement with numerous clients and lots of new, interesting, and different problems to solve. Funny enough, technical presales seemed to be a logical fit. I was very good in front of an audience. As a consultant, I had given dozens of technical presentations. The idea of "parachuting" in to see a customer, making a technical pitch, and then "helicoptering" out was very appealing. And I loved the idea of being more in control of my income. This, of course, is the result of being on a commission plan. As a sales engineer there was significant upside in terms of what I could earn. I was a little intimidated at first by the uncertainty of a commission plan, but also very intrigued.

So back to my first story. I'm at the cocktail party. I had just recently started this new role as an SE, and a gentleman, whom I've not met before, asks me what I do for a living. I respond saying that I have just recently joined a software company, adding that I was an expert in a field called *Enterprise Architecture*: a field that few people had heard of, much less understood. I'm quite certain I went to unnecessary lengths attempting to explain to him what EA was, and why companies should care, etc. (Come to think of it I'm a bit surprised he didn't excuse himself at that point.). Nonetheless, I concluded my long-winded answer by saying, *"Actually I just moved into a new role. I'm now responsible for giving product demonstrations in the context of sales engagements."* With that his face lit up a little and he said, *"Oh! So, you're in software sales!"* I think my first thought was *"Did he not hear what I just explained to him about what EA was? Did he not just hear me explain to him that I'm the technical expert? What's wrong with this guy?"* But in the interest of being cordial, and in pure improv style, I didn't miss a beat. *"Yes. Exactly. I'm in software sales. Why didn't I say that?!"* I said smiling. Thankfully, for both of us, we were interrupted by a mutual friend and the conversation moved on.

That conversation rattled around in my head the rest of the night. The more I thought about his response, the more I came to realize that he was RIGHT. I WAS in software sales. That IS my primary job now. I just never actually thought about it that way until he said what he said. I never actually thought of myself as "being in sales." To be sure, I have a different role than that of the "typical sales professional". My responsibility is different in the context of a software sales engagement. But at the end of the day, I'm in software sales. From that moment on, until this very day, whenever anyone asks me what I do for a living, the very first words out of my mouth are *"I'm in software sales."*

• • •

The second story took place only a few months later. My company was hosting a user event in the Washington DC area. We had upwards of about 100+ people in attendance. I was still one of the new guys but beginning to establish myself—at least so I thought. I was invited to participate in the event and was asked to give a 20-30-minute product demonstration during the afternoon session. The software product that I had been hired to support, the software product that I was the self-proclaimed expert on, had been recently acquired by the company and, as such, was new to their existing customer base. Because I was the so-called expert, this was an opportunity to introduce the audience to this new concept, technology, and platform.

To say the very least, I was incredibly excited for the invitation to speak at the event. It was my first opportunity to speak to a large audience since I had joined this new company. And, to be able to do so in front of my peers, and colleagues was an opportunity I relished.

There I am, the day of the event. The room was packed. We had a highly engaged audience. I was ready for my time to shine under the spotlight. My speaking slot finally arrived, and I took the stage. I opened with a few slides and then launched into my demo. I had numerous items that I wanted to demonstrate, but very limited on time. I knew I had to be efficient, and focused. I showed a multitude of screens. I flowed from one view to the next, and man, was I smooth. I think I might have covered more ground in 20 minutes than I typically would in 40. I navigated through that demo like a seasoned expert. The mouse and my words flowed in perfect harmony. I finished right on time, and handed the stage back to the event facilitator, quietly congratulating myself for a rock star performance as I walked off stage.

A few hours later, after we had finished cleaning up from the event, I found myself alone on the elevator with one of the top sales managers. He didn't know me very well yet, and there was a moment of awkward silence – which I decided to break. *"So, what did you think of the event?"* He turned slightly, without really looking at me, and muttered *"It was OK."* The awkward silence returned, now thicker than before. Determined not to give up, I tried again. *"And what did you think of my brief presentation?"* Thinking to myself, certainly this will get a positive response from him. After all, my session was one of the best all day. I was polished. Nothing crashed. I got through all my material. I finished on time. What's not to like? Instead, he now turns, looks at me dead on, and says, *"Honestly Chris, I don't think anyone in there had any idea what you were talking about."*

He wouldn't have caught me more off guard if he had turned and poured a bucket of cold water on my head. I was flabbergasted to hear that response, completely and totally caught off guard. It's a moment I will never forget. It was in that moment that I realized I had a LOT to learn about technical presales. Being able to move a mouse, and talk at the same time in front of an audience was NOT the recipe for success; that was just the most basic skill needed, the "ticket to enter" if you will, but nowhere near a seat in the front row.

Apparently, I had some things to learn about sales. In fact, I recall one day a few weeks later, and still clearly new to the role, one of my sales counterparts said something to the effect of the "sales process." I remember thinking *"Process? There's a process to sales?"* I thought we just showed up and made a pitch. If they liked it, they bought and if not, they didn't, end of story. I was a very naive engineer when I first got into this role.

The point is, I did have a lot to learn to become an effective presales engineer. And so, the journey to success, through trial and error, began. Over the course of the next five years I gave hundreds of demos. I discovered what worked, and what didn't. I learned from my successes, and I grew through my failures. I became one of the most highly sought-after technical presales resources in the company – in my particular domain, of course. I was regularly invited to present at user conferences, and other industry events. I exceeded quota and made president's club every year I was eligible. I learned from great mentors and great colleagues. At one point along the way, I found myself working longer, and longer hours. I wanted to be successful, but not at the expense of my personal life. So, after discovering what it took to be effective, I then searched and found ways to be more efficient with my time as well. I discovered what it took to be both highly effective, and efficient.

I share all this with you not to brag, quite the contrary. I share this with you because you would have to search far, and wide to find someone who was more confused about what his role was, more blissfully and wrongfully overconfident, and more clueless about what it took to be a highly effective, and successful sales engineer than when I first got into the business. I took some hard lumps. I had to swallow my pride. And I had to figure it out. But after years of trial and error, and experience in the field, and years of watching other sales engineers both succeed and fail, I discovered a formula that worked.

• • •

Fast forward to the year 2011. I was with a new company, a small software company based in London. I had taken over responsibility for a small team of pre- and post-sales consultants. After sitting through a handful of software demos given by the team in my first few weeks, I quickly discovered that they were making a lot of the same mistakes I had made when I first got into the business. They were all VERY good with the software. They were technical experts, like I had been, when I first got into the job. They also didn't really understand the role of technical presales. Again, much like me in the early days. They weren't even aware of some of things they were doing that were potentially detrimental to a sales engagement. They certainly were not aware of some of the specific techniques that they needed to employ to give themselves and their sales counterparts the best opportunity to win the deal, much less their customers the opportunity to make the best decision possible.

Allow me to be very clear. They weren't bad at their jobs. But there was a lot of room for improvement – for their own job satisfaction, for their own benefit, for the benefit of the team and the company, and for the benefit of the customers and prospects they were working with. They just needed some training and coaching, and as such, the content you have in your hands was born.

I discovered that there were a set of patterns that, when followed, predicted technical presales success with incredible accuracy. I will go into more detail on how that success is measured later. What's most important to understand right now is that these patterns that I discovered are teachable, learnable, and applicable, regardless of your background, education, personality and/or speaking style.

Over the years, these patterns evolved into the Six Habits of Highly Effective Sales Engineers. They can be applied by anyone in this business with astonishing results. Read on and get ready to change the way you approach technical presales forever.

Acknowledgement

There are a number of people that have helped me on my journey that I would like to recognize and thank.

I want to thank Anthony Spadafore, creator of Pathfinders, who counseled me years ago and helped me discover my innate, God-given talents. The turning point in my career that launched me into technical presales.

I want to thank Eric Shott and Jim Lee. The two men who hired me into my first presales job. Thank you for the coaching, patience and guidance.

I want to thank all the sales professionals I've had the privilege of working with and for over the years. I'm not going to name names, because I would run out of space, but you know who you are.

I want to thank all the other sales engineers I've had the opportunity to work with and learn from.

I want to thank Mike Levine for giving me the opportunity to share my message on a bigger stage.

I want to thank Drew Clyde and Jack O'Donnell and the Leesburg Junction for hosting my first ever public seminar. That was a turning point for me.

I want to thank John Estrella for the coaching and encouragement. Thanks for the PUSH!

Most of all, I want to thank all the customers I've had the opportunity to present to and work with over the years. You are the reason I love this profession.

#THESIXHABITSOFHESE

INTRODUCTION

Who is this book for?

This book is for anyone in technical sales, whether that's enterprise software sales, complex platform sales, technology services, etc. If your sales cycles or sales opportunities require the involvement of sales engineers – to give software demonstrations, make technical presentations, design technical solutions, etc. – this book is for you. Whether you *are* a sales engineer, *depend* on sales engineers to close business, or *manage* sales teams that include sales engineers, you will benefit from this book.

How do I define sales engineer? Anyone who is in what the industry commonly refers to as *technical presales* fits into this category. Traditionally, these are the engineers and technical experts within a software company that give product demonstrations in the context of a sales opportunity.

You may or may not think of yourself as a sales engineer. You might not have the title of sales engineer. But if you give software demonstrations for a living or provide technical support to sales professionals in the context of sales opportunities, you fall into this category. Other titles and roles that fit into this category are:

- Solution Architect
- Sales Consultant
- Value Engineer
- Solution Designer
- Sales Evangelist
- Application Engineer

For clarification, I will use the acronym SE when referring to a sales engineer, and any one of the above roles, throughout the book.

This book is especially written for those of you who have recently moved into the role. Once, an attendee of one of my seminars, who was a seasoned SE, told me, "I only wish I had heard this when I started my career at 24." If you have just entered the profession this book is a gold mine for you. Or maybe you are considering a career in technical presales. If so, the book in your hand will give you great insight into what this role is all about.

This book is also for anyone in software sales. If you sell a technical product – software, services and solutions, and you work with and/or depend on technical resources to close business and generate revenue, this book is for you. It will give you insight into how we (SEs) think and operate. If your team is underperforming, you have in your hands a wealth of information that will drastically improve the way you and your team operate, present, demo and deliver. Incidentally, as you read through the book, you will see that it is written as if I'm speaking to a sales engineer. You will see references to "your sales counterpart" or "sales rep". That would be you.

This book is also for those of you in sales and SE management. I'll assume that you and/or your organization have defined your own sales processes, best practices, sales motions, etc. You've probably implemented sales training, sales coaching, sales enablement and onboarding. Here's the thing. SEs are a unique breed. I suspect I'm preaching to the choir with that statement. They require a unique brand of sales training. Yet, there is very little sales training in the market designed specifically for SEs. The material you have in your hands will do wonders to augment the training and enablement you currently have for your SEs and will help you build cohesion between your sales teams and SEs like you never imagined.

Introducing the Six Habits

Taking a page out of, *"Great Demo!"* by Peter Cohan, I'm going to do the last thing first. That's right, I'm going to answer the most important question right now. What are The Six Habits of Highly Effective Sales Engineers?

1. Partner – Habit #1 is to partner with your sales counterpart. To think of your relationship with your sales counterpart as a partnership. Sales is a team sport, and you are on the same team. In this section, we will examine the different perspectives each player brings to the table, identify some mistakes to avoid, and offer a process for collaboration.

2. Probe – Habit #2 is to probe into any request for a demonstration. It is the habit of digging into a customers' objectives, requirements, expectations, etc. We do this by hosting a Technical Discovery Call, which we will discuss at great length. In the section, I will provide specific guidance on how to execute technical discovery, offer a list of questions you can use, and discuss other important clues to be on the lookout for that will shape how and what you demonstrate.

3. Prepare – Habit #3 is to prepare with effectiveness and efficiency in mind. This requires a very keen understanding of the difference between preparing demo content vs. preparing the demo script or story. In this chapter, I will reveal the most common mistakes SEs make and time wasters that interfere with preparing for demos. We'll walk through a plan for how to stay laser focused.

4. Practice – Habit #4 is the easiest in nature, but too important to leave out. The most consistently successful SE's practice their demos religiously. They understand that technical issues in a demo can delay or crush a deal. Before a demo, they make sure to "click every click." In this section, I will unveil the one thing you don't want after a click and offer specific tips for what to look for when "spot checking" your demos.

5. Perform – Habit #5 is to perform under the spotlight. The most successful SE's understand that a demo is more than a technical presentation, it's a performance. There are very specific things that we need to do, say, and avoid in order to earn the trust of your customers and the respect of your colleagues. In this chapter I will arm you with 20 specific tips and, techniques and best practices that will elevate you to technical presales superstar status.

6. Perfect – Habit #6 is to consistently perfect your trade. It's based on the principle of constant improvement. Top performing SE's consistently seek to learn and improve. They collaborate with their sales counterparts and constantly evaluate their performance.

#thesixhabitsofhese

Before you launch into the book, if you would like to follow our posts on LinkedIn related to The Six Habits – or post any thoughts of your own as you journey through the book, I encourage you to follow and or tag the hashtag #thesixhabitsofhese.

Enjoy the read!

Figure 1. The Six Habits of Highly Effective Sales Engineers

How this book is organized?

The chapters of this book address each one of the habits in detail. In the next chapter, we will look at what it means to partner with our sales counterparts. We will explore what individuals with different roles bring to the table, identify some mistakes to avoid, and offer a process for collaboration. In Chapter 3, we will discuss the Technical Discovery Call at length, and provide specific guidance on how to execute, offer a suggested list of questions, and discuss other important clues to be on the lookout for. Chapter 4 tackles how best to prepare for efficiency and effectiveness. I will reveal the most common mistakes and time wasters that interfere with preparing for demos and give you a plan for how to be laser focused.

In Chapter 5, the shortest chapter in the book, I will elaborate on what I mean by "click every click," and offer specific tips on what to look for when "spot checking" your demos. I will also unveil the one thing you don't want after a click. Habit #5 is the longest section of the book and for many of you, may prove to be your favorite. It is divided into two chapters.

In Chapter 6 and 7 we will cover 20 specific tips, techniques and best practices that enable you to perform like a technical presales superstar on stage. Your customers will appreciate you. Your colleagues will respect you. And once you master these skills, your calendar will stay consistently full. In Chapter 8, we close out the discussion on the Six Habits by discussing the importance of consistently, and constantly striving to perfect your demo. It involves collaborating with your sales counterparts after the fact to evaluate the customer meeting and make improvements with every opportunity.

Each of the habits are incredibly powerful, and impactful in and of themselves, but the magic of the Six Habits is the integration, and the interdependency between them because they all relate to, and build upon, one another.

CHAPTER 1

YOU ARE IN SALES

What is the goal of Technical Presales?

I ask this because there seems to be a lot of confusion, and disagreement about what the primary objective of the role really is. In fact, when I speak at an event or teach a class, I often ask this question to level-set with the audience. I regularly get some very interesting answers. "To provide technical support to sales," some people will say. "To provide technical answers." "To show and demonstrate complex technical solutions." All of these are legitimate answers, since they are all part of the role, and then some. But the number one goal—our MAIN objective as sales engineers, what we are ultimately responsible for, and what we will use for the basis of this book—is to get (what I like to refer to as) the TECHNICAL WIN.

What's the *Technical Win*?

The technical win is to convince the prospect that your solution will meet their needs, solve their problems, and help them achieve their objectives. (By solution, I mean software, platform, tools, etc.) What does technical presales not entail? Your job as a technical presales engineer is not to teach your prospects how to use our software. It is not training. It is not to solve all of a prospects' problems. It is not your job, or responsibility to show them "everything about everything" when it comes to the product you are selling. It is simply to show them – no, CONVINCE them – that your software, solutions, and company will meet their requirements, solve their problems, and enable them to achieve their desired outcomes.

Many of us in this role come from a technical background. Many of us come from a problem-solving role whether we were in customer success, post-sales consulting, training, or expert users of the software. We are used to playing the role of technical expert. We are used to solving problems. Here's the thing, however, we are no longer in the problem-solving business; we are in the *convincing* business. This requires different muscles, different skills, and different approaches.

How does this differ from the role of the salesperson that we are paired up with? If we are responsible for the technical win, what is their job? What is their role? They are ultimately responsible for revenue. That's it. Very simply put, they are responsible for revenue and you are responsible for the technical win. For them, this includes things like managing the account, negotiating price, working out terms, closing the deal, etc. They are essentially responsible for the overarching sales process, which includes prospecting, by the way, something very few people like. They are also responsible for the account, the opportunity, and the customer relationship, the last of which we play a large role in, of course. But, at the end of the day, we own the technical win. Does that include answering technical questions? Yes, of course. Does that include making technical presentations and, demonstrations, of course. However, success in this role is ultimately measured by one thing: getting the customer to say YES.

INSIGHT: *In the late stages of completing this book, I had the opportunity to discuss this term "the technical win" with John Care, Author of Mastering Technical Sales: The Sales Engineer's Handbook. He's one of the foremost experts in this space. He* shared with me that he dislikes the term as it's "*hard to measure and can encourage an SE to disconnect before the business win happens*". He went on to say that "*no one gets paid on the technical win*". He argues that effective SEs hold themselves accountable for the business win as well. It occurred to me that even though I use the term "technical win", I'm in complete agreement with him. By no means am I suggesting that we, as sales engineers, should be focused solely on the technology. Quite the contrary, as you will see throughout the book, I'm emphatic about aligning whatever technology you represent with the business needs and objectives of your prospects and customers. A key aspect of the "technical win", in fact, an addendum to the definition above, is "to convince your prospects that the business value of the solution outweighs or justifies the investment".

I use the term 'technical win' throughout this book. I do so because so many of the SEs I have observed seem to forget that we are not in this role simply to inform and educate. Our job – as we will discuss in great detail – is to convince. Please understand that when I use this term – technical win – I'm referring to the responsibility to both convince the audience of the technical superiority of the solution and establish the business value of the investment.

What are our goals personally?

So, if the goal of presales is to get the *technical win*, what is our goal? What I mean is, what are our personal goals and objectives? What do we individually hope to accomplish in the role?

I can't speak for everyone in this role, of course, nor do I want to put words in your mouth but allow me to share with you what I've observed and experienced over the years.

Number one, and I think, unanimously, we want to maximize our income. Our pay is usually based on the number of deals we win. So, we, of course want to close as many deals as possible. We want our presentations/demonstrations to be a positive experience – for ourselves, our colleagues and our audiences. We want the audience to understand what it is they are seeing. We want them to be impressed and of course like what they see. We want them walking away convinced that our people, products, and solutions would solve their problems and meet their needs. We want them walking away ready to buy our software.

We also want to maximize our time and minimize unnecessary late nights and long hours. We want to avoid "sprints to the finish line" preparing for demos and customer meetings. Thus, we want ample time to prepare effectively for customer meetings and presentations.

INSIGHT: *I personally didn't want to have to work late nights, on a consistent basis, in order to succeed, but there was a stretch of time that I did – a long stretch of time. UNTIL I figured out how to be both efficient and effective with my time and avoid working on demo content that I'd never have time to show anyways. We will cover this a great deal in Chapter 4.*

Finally, we never want to feel like we're wasting our time, whether that's preparing for or traveling to a demo that's poorly qualified or seems unwinnable. We don't want to feel as though we're being asked to demonstrate something that's beyond our capabilities, or those of the software or platform.

This sounds reasonable...

This sounds reasonable enough, right? To achieve the technical win, and to meet our own objectives? This doesn't sound like an impossible task... Right?

Think again. This is not an easy job. We are put, at times, in impossible situations. We can find ourselves caught between sales teams stressed to close business, looking for you to work magic with the software. Product teams juggling hundreds of requirements, expecting you to demonstrate the software with precision. Prospects and customers, looking to you for answers and holding you accountable when things don't work – be it right or wrong. We are on the front line with prospects and customers, and often so much is riding on the software demonstrations we give – for us, our colleagues and our customers.

But when we succeed, we're superheroes. When we give an "out of the park" demo (that's a baseball reference for home run, in case any of you aren't baseball fans), it's exhilarating. In fact, I'm quite convinced that that's why those of us in this profession stay. It's the thrill of the hunt, so to speak. The thrill of being presented with a challenging set of requirements to address and delivering the ideal demo. But if there's anything I've learned in this business, there are very few "instruction manuals" on how to be a successful sales engineer.

So how do we do this? How do we achieve the technical win and meet our own objectives? And how do we do it on a consistent, reliable, and predictable basis? The book you're holding in your hands, of course, is going to walk step by step through the six habits just introduced. But before we get into that, let's just answer this question notionally. How do we achieve the technical win?

It begins by establishing trust and building confidence with our audience – that is, the prospects and/or customers that we are working with. As a rule of thumb, we are going to be given the benefit of the doubt in most cases, because we're the "technical expert," and not the "sales guy." But at the same time, we must earn it. We must earn their trust and confidence.

We need to build relationships and develop rapport. We do this by listening to, and understanding their objectives, goals, requirements, etc. We offer insights and suggestions. We demonstrate our knowledge, and competencies around their areas of concern and interest through presenting the product and solution. More specifically, by demonstrating the capabilities that explicitly address their need and solve their problems. We show our audiences how they can achieve success using our solutions by giving them a vision of hope for the future. We ultimately get the technical win by getting our audience excited by generating enthusiasm for what's possible.

Seems straight forward enough, right? What's the problem? We know the goal of technical presales – to get the technical win. We know what we need to do to get there. What are the obstacles that get in the way of our success? Why aren't we able to achieve this every time?

What gets in the way?

There are numerous things that stand in the way of our success and throw us off course. Let's review a few of those things. Probably the biggest obstacle to our success is finding ourselves in a customer situation we are ill-prepared for. The best example of this is when we've been asked, or even forced to do a demo, or presentation that we are unprepared to give. But why and/or how does that happen?

Sometimes our sales counterparts don't properly qualify for an opportunity or a customer request. Maybe we simply aren't given enough time to prepare or maybe a given solution is oversold by marketing or sales. Maybe we misinterpreted the expectations and requirements or didn't ask the right questions to begin with. Sometimes the prospect misrepresents their needs, requirements and/or expectations. Whatever the case, if we find ourselves unprepared in any given situation, it indicates that there was a form of miscommunication somewhere, possibly between sales rep, sales engineer and/or prospect.

Regardless of where that disconnect occurs, all these issues are addressable, and avoidable. We will address all these situations so that you will be armed with the skills necessary to avoid being caught off guard or ill-prepared. And in the unlikely event that you are, how to handle it with grace and confidence, and keep a deal alive.

What are some of the other reasons we fail to achieve our objective? What are some of the other obstacles that get in the way of a successful demonstration and hurt our deals? Sometimes new, unexpected people appear – either in the context of a given meeting or in the context of the overall sales engagement. They introduce new ideas, new priorities, needs, etc. And as a result, it derails or delays the deal and/or throws the sales presentation or demo into a tailspin. Sometimes we come face to face with antagonists who seem to care only about making us and our solutions look dumb. Sometimes we have technical difficulties during the context of a sales demonstration, and when that happens – which is inevitable, by the way – we need to know how to roll with the punches. Sometimes the demo just misses the mark and the prospect isn't impressed. It happens. It's part of being in technical presales, but again, we need to know how to handle those situations as well. Sometimes there's a personality clash and we just don't click with the audience. Again, we need to recognize those situations and be prepared.

At the end of the day there are numerous things that can and will go wrong in the context of a sales opportunity, and more specifically a software demonstration. Things that may seem to be outside of our control. But the reality is we may have far more influence and control over those things than it might appear on the surface. By learning and adopting these six habits and the related skills, you'll be equipped to avoid many of those scenarios and manage every situation.

What mistakes do we make?

What is it that we do that gets in the way of our own success? We've cited the obstacles that get in the way. But sometimes we are our own worst enemy. The good news is that these are the easiest issues to address – because they are well within our control. These are the biggest mistakes I've seen made in this profession. (And frankly, the mistakes I've made and had to learn from over the years).

1. First and foremost, we don't understand our role. We think of ourselves as engineers, as technologists. We don't think of ourselves as sales.

2. We focus on the wrong things. We focus on ourselves, our products, our features, our story, etc. etc. etc. (Are you seeing a trend here? It's the "me, me, me" syndrome!) We need to focus first on our prospects and customers – their objectives, their needs, their requirements. Then position our solutions accordingly.

3. We also focus too much on the *thing* and not the *story*, i.e., the product and not the message.

4. We confuse presales for training. We come by this honestly. Many of us come from a consulting or technical support background. We are used to providing training on software tools. But a sales demonstration is NOT training. The goal is NOT to teach the audience how to use the tool. It's to get them excited. It's to show them what's possible. It's to get them to say yes.

5. We confuse technical presales with consulting. We make the mistake of trying to solve a prospects' problems as if we've already been hired.

6. We dive too deeply into their problems – especially in the context of preparing for a product demonstration. We forget to leave full problem solving to the post-sales consultants.

7. We treat every customer or opportunity the same. We approach every demo the same. In technical presales one size

does not fit all. Every customer is different. Every situation is unique. What makes one prospect say YES may be very different from what will make another say yes.

8. We take too long to prepare for demos. We get carried away and build more than is required. We insist on showing customers unnecessary content and capabilities because they're cool or because we built them. It delays deals. Derails conversations. And alienates our sales counterparts.

9. We overlook the little things – such as practice. We forget to double check that everything is working. As a result, we have a crash or failure in front of a customer – usually at the worst possible time. Something that could easily have been avoided had we just spot checked our demo.

10. We've not been taught the skills that turn a technical demonstration into a winning sales demonstration. In fact, some of us don't recognize they exist when we enter this field. (I didn't.)

11. We don't learn from our mistakes, or at least learn from what went wrong, from one demo to the next. We accept weaknesses and limitations in our software without finding a work-around.

That probably seems like a long list of issues, challenges, and obstacles to deal with. We are going to deal with all of them. It begins with changing our mindset.

You Are in Sales!

Yes, my friends, if you are a sales engineer, you are in sales. As we discussed a moment ago, you may have a different title – solution architect, sales consultant, value engineer, etc. But regardless of your title, if you are responsible for technical presales presentations and demonstrations, you are in sales.

Why is this so important? Why do I even take the time to mention this? Because so many of the people I have worked with over the years – in fact, so many people I've seen in this role – do not think of themselves as sales. Nothing, however, could be further from the truth. And worse, nothing could be more detrimental to your success. If you have a quota, you are in sales. If your job is to convince people to select your software over another, you are in sales.

I just have a hard time with that word Chris – "sales"

I know you do. I did too! For many of us, the idea that we are in sales simply goes against our constitutional compass. We're engineers at heart. We're engineers in the way we think. Like I said in my opening, sales is almost offensive. But allow me to stress, I'm not saying you're a used car salesman, who does whatever and says whatever to get the sale. What I'm saying is in order for us to truly succeed in this role, we need to change our mindset. We need to clearly recognize that we are no longer in the teaching/consulting/informing business. We are in the *convincing* business.

We have a different role from that of our sales counterparts, and we'll talk about that a great deal in this book. But if you are in this role, or you are considering a job in the field, please know that yes, you are in sales. Just as I discovered, almost accidentally at a cocktail party, that was my job. If you don't come to grips with this fact, adopting the six habits is like building a house on a shaky foundation.

Sales is a Courtship

Let's go a step further. What exactly does it mean to be in sales? Sales is a courtship. We need to interact with prospects and customers the same way we would if we were courting someone –

because that's EXACTLY what we are doing! If you're married or in a long-term relationship, I want you to think back to your first couple of dates. Did you act then the way you do now? Of course not! And how did you act differently?

Here are some guidelines:

1. We ALWAYS put our best foot forward – with respect to ourselves, our solutions, and our company.
2. We ALWAYS act on our best behavior. We use our best manners.
3. We ALWAYS represent the company, our software, and our colleagues in the highest regard.
4. We NEVER air our dirty laundry – whether about our company, the product, our colleagues, etc.

You might be saying to yourself, why would you even mention these things? They seem so obvious. So basic. My answer: you would not believe how many times I've attended a demonstration in which the sales engineer was grumpy about something – the company, his sales counterparts, the product, etc. and made his/her disapproval known openly and often. I've seen sales engineers get belligerent with prospects. I've seen them get defensive, rude, arrogant, insulted by questions, etc. etc. The list frankly goes on and on. We are in sales. We are guests in someone else's place of business. And we need to act accordingly – for our own benefit! Remember, our goal is to get the Technical Win.

CHAPTER 2

HABIT #1 - PARTNER

Sales engineers rarely, if ever, work sales opportunities in isolation. As a sale engineer, you will be paired up with one or more sales reps. The quality of your relationship with your "sales counterparts", will determine, to a great degree, your job satisfaction and the team's overall success. If you are paired with a single sales rep, the two of you will work in tandem to identify, qualify, advance, and, ideally, close business. This is the model made famous by IBM. An account manager was assigned a sales engineer, and the two worked side by side to manage and execute sales opportunities. It's a model that still exists today in many organizations.

You may be assigned to a group of reps that can call on you at any time, regularly pulling you in different directions. You might also find yourself in a matrixed organization, in which case you're one of a pool of resources that any sales rep with a specific requirement can call on. Regardless of the situation, or structure of your organization, your ability to collaborate with your sales counterparts and the quality of those relationships, will, to a large degree, dictate your success.

The first habit of highly effective SEs is to PARTNER with your sales counterparts. Treat these relationships as *partnerships*.

The most successful SEs understand that they are in sales and recognize their role on the team. They understand that not unlike other partnerships – such as a marriage – it requires collaboration, give and take, negotiation, communication, etc.

In this chapter, we're going to break this down and first look at what an effective partnership looks like. Fact is, these partnerships can be difficult. We'll discuss why that is and consider some of the fundamental differences between ourselves and our sales counterparts. Sometimes they do things that disrupt the relationship, but so do we. We will examine some of the common mistakes that we make and how to avoid them. We will then walk through the three fundamental aspects of developing this habit. First, recognizing that sales is a team sport. Second, the importance of clarifying roles and responsibilities. Third, the value of establishing an integrated sales-presales process and how to go about setting one up.

The Profile of an Effective Partnership

What does an effective partnership between sales engineer and sales even look like? Are there specific characteristics that can be readily, commonly identified that indicate partnership effectiveness? A resounding yes. Like all relationships, they will have different dynamics. Each one is unique. But below is a list of the most common aspects of a well-functioning partnership – the profile of an effective sales-SE partnership, if you will.

- Goals and objectives are clarified and aligned
- Effective communication between them
- Mutual respect for one another
- Division of roles and responsibilities established and clarified
- Each party takes responsibility for their part of a sale
- Clear expectations on a consistent basis
- A feedback loop has been built into the sales process
- Prioritize the customer and opportunity over personal agenda

- Show loyalty to the company, the product, and one another
- Proactively engage one another and their customers

Does that sound like an effective partnership to you? Does it sound like the type of working relationship that would enable you to succeed? Do you currently have working relationships like the one described here? What are the things you could be doing differently to develop this kind of partnership? Before we answer those questions, let's consider why this is so difficult to begin with.

These Partnerships Can be Difficult

This might seem so obvious – to partner with our sales counterparts. Why is this so hard? Why does this not happen naturally to begin with? The reality is that there are some fundamental differences in the way we think – sales engineers and sales reps. There are fundamental differences in the way we approach opportunities and customer engagements. Although we have the same overarching goal, we tend to have different objectives individually. We have different perspectives on how to engage with a client, an opportunity, or even a sales meeting. If we're not careful and intentional with the way we approach the relationship, these differences can easily get in the way of a cohesive team and can create conflict.

How are we different?

Stealing the name of a very well-known book by John Gray, PhD, it's not a stretch to say that *sales reps are from Mars and SEs are from Venus*. (No, I'm not suggesting that sales reps are all men and SEs are all women.) What I'm saying is that we tend to be so different in the way we think – the way we're wired – sometimes it *is* as if we're from different planets. Let's compare how we tend to approach a sales opportunity.

Consider the *time to prepare*. We typically want ample time to prepare. We typically don't want to rush right in and give a demo without some information. Our sales counterparts on the other hand are eager to schedule the demo as soon as possible. They want to strike while the iron is hot.

What about the *content and scope of a demo*? It's in our best interest to have a focused demo with limited scope and requirements. Our sales counterparts? They often want to go in and show as many things as possible, in hopes that something will stick.

What about the *number of people in the room*? I've always preferred as small and focused an audience as possible. That helps keep the conversation and demo narrow and focused. Our sales counterparts often want as many people in the room as possible.

What about how we *describe our capabilities*? Salespeople typically want to say YES to everything. *"Sure, we can do that! Absolutely, we can support that."* Us? We prefer to be more precise with our answers. We don't want to oversell the solution. We don't want to set ourselves for failure downstream. Salespeople tend to have shorter-term perspective – let's just make the sale. We tend to have a longer-term perspective – let's make sure the solution will work as projected.

What about *fear*? The thing we tend to fear the most is losing credibility and/or steering the client wrong – or at least feeling like we've done so. Our sales counterparts? They (typically) fear losing the deal over all else.

Incidentally, I *fear* I may be angering some readers at this point with some of these comments. It may sound as though I am being highly critical of or don't like sales reps. Nothing could be further from the truth. First, some of my best friends are sales reps. Second, I'm exaggerating a little to make a point. And by no means am I saying that all sales reps think the way I'm suggesting above. But from my experience, these do tend to be some of the common differences.

Sometimes sales reps make claims that are difficult for us to demonstrate, or worse beyond the true capabilities of the tool. That puts us in a very difficult place. We don't want to make them look bad. But we also don't want to oversell the solution or overstate what is and is not possible. So, this requires some finesse.

In fact, let's address this one now, because this is important. What are some ways in which you can diffuse a situation in which a salesperson has oversold a solution or overstated what the software can do? The following is a list of statements that you can make to downplay and redirect the conversation without making anyone look bad:

- *What Bill said is true under certain circumstances, but given what you are trying to do...*
- *What Jason said is partially true, but the other side of the coin is...*
- *The fundamentals of what Mary said are true, but there are some specifics that may need clarification.*

What have we done here? First and foremost, we are being respectful to our sales counterparts. We're not throwing them under the bus. We're not saying *No, that's not right.* We're acknowledging the point they were trying to make. But then clarifying the point for the customer or prospect so we haven't left them with an expectation that the software cannot live up to.

INSIGHT: *To be sure I'm oversimplifying and generalizing here, but I do so to make a point. We tend to be driven more by our engineering background than our desire to close a deal. We value clarity, expertise, precision, etc. Sales reps are driven more by their sales background and their responsibility to generate revenue.*

They undervalue us. We undervalue them.

These differences can drive a wedge between the very two colleagues that depend on one another the *most*. In most cases, deals would not be won without the support of talented SEs to get the technical win and help establish the business value. And we (SEs) certainly wouldn't be hitting any quotas without our sales counterparts to close the deal. However, sometimes we will be taken for granted. I've seen some SEs get disgruntled over the fact that the sales reps "make the big bucks".

In fact, I've seen some circumstances where when the deal was won, the account manager thought it was all them. Or in their mind, it was the product that just sold itself, and they dismiss or overlook the role the SE played. Yet, it may very well be the SE who gets unfairly blamed if a deal goes south. (By the way, the opposite is also true, in fact, mostly true in my case. The salespeople that I've had the privilege of working with over the years highly recognize and appreciate the value of their SEs.)

However, if we're fully honest with ourselves, there are times that we undervalue them. We tend to think of ourselves as the "smart ones." We think "what would they do without us?" I will caution you if you've ever had this kind of perspective. It's a very different skill set to go "knocking on doors", chasing prospects, leaving countless voice mails, sending multiple emails – just to get a meeting. Putting yourself out there day in and day out, knowing that you are going to face rejection on a daily basis is not easy.

Meanwhile, we're the expert who's invited in to be the "knight in shining armor". We're that person that prospects tend to trust and look up to as the technical expert. I guarantee you there are sales reps that envy our position. We have very different skill sets, with very different roles, so I caution you about judging. Until or unless you have actually "carried a bag" as they say and worked in a pure sales role, it's easy to underestimate just how difficult that role is.

From my experience, most sales reps earn every penny they make. As do we.

Got it. We're fundamentally different. What's the point?

The point is that in spite of these differences, we need to think of our sales counterparts as partners, and take responsibility for making the relationship work. I've worked with some sales reps who want to just go out and talk to anyone about anything – and drag me along in the process. OK, so I'm exaggerating a little bit, but I'm trying to make a point. Some sales folks are so desperate for business, they're happy to have the opportunity to speak to just about anyone. They just want to "get in there and show them something." However, as an SE, I always wanted to be a little more selective. My time is valuable. For me to just "go in and have a conversation" meant prep time, travel time, etc. So, I didn't just agree to any demo request. There's a discussion – a negotiation if you will, that needs to take place. But how do we do this? And how do we do it and avoid the most common mistakes along the way?

What Mistakes Do WE Make?

First let's consider the opposite – to think of the relationship with our sales counterparts as adversarial. When we do, we will treat them as adversaries. We develop an "us vs. them" mentality. We think of them as the opposition. Clearly this is a bad foundation for a sales team.

Say YES to Everything

Is it possible to be too accommodating? Yes, it is. Another mistake we make is we allow ourselves to become doormats. We get stepped on, "used and abused", because we agree to every request for a demo or support. It's flattering to be wanted and needed. It's certainly a complement to be highly sought after by sales folks. And I don't blame the sales reps for wanting to bring in the best resources for each and every deal. They are highly motivated and incentivized to close deals. But we need to know when to say NO.

We become Roadblocks

On the flip side, we sometimes develop the reputation for being roadblocks. If we always show resistance to requests for demos, we may be considered difficult to work with. To avoid that, I recommend you treat every demo request with an open mind. Listen to the requirements. What is the scenario? What is the customer is trying to do? How big and urgent is the opportunity, etc. It may or may not be something that you can prioritize. But at least you have received it with an open mind, and if you don't have the bandwidth, maybe you can find someone else or provide some support.

INSIGHT: I recently had the opportunity to speak with Rob Falcone, Author of "Just F*ing Demo". On the topic of becoming roadblocks, he had this valuable insight to share:

"Having spent time as an SE and sales rep, I've been on both sides of the "do we or don't we demo?" tug of war. Understand that this common friction can not only put the deal in jeopardy but will add unnecessary stress to your life! When this scenario inevitably arises, I've found it effective to step back and ask myself "why?" I'm feeling resistant to the demo. Maybe I feel the deal isn't qualified. Maybe I don't have sufficient requirements to build the demo. Once I can pinpoint why I'm resistant, I can work with the sales rep to address THAT in a way that not only eliminates stress, but also moves the deal forward."

Great advice! Thanks Rob!

The mistake that I see people make is when an account manager requests a demo and the sales engineer says flat out NO, without taking into consideration the request, the account, the deal size, etc. If you instantly decline requests like that, you may very well develop a bad reputation and may soon find that no one wants to bring you into their deals.

What's the Solution?

So, what are we to do? How do we adopt and develop Habit #1 to PARTNER with our sales counterparts? There are three things we need to do, a) get your mindset right, b) clarify roles and responsibilities, and c) follow a process.

Sales is a Team Sport

The first thing we need to do to develop this habit is to change our mindset. *Sales is a team sport.* It is not an individual sport. Yes, you are going to be looked at for individual performance. You will very likely not have a team of people reporting to you. However, you need to think of yourself as part of a team, particularly those of you who sell enterprise software, or complex technical solutions. The more complex the technology or broad the solution, the more likely you will find yourself working with multiple sales reps. You might even find yourself working with multiple sales engineers—each with a different expertise or specialty.

Like any team sport, the different positions have different responsibilities that require different skills. As such, sales engineers, and the sales folks we are paired with, bring unique skills to the table. The effective merging and meshing of those skills produce the most sales, generate the most revenue, and deliver the most beneficial outcomes for customers.

Clarifying roles and responsibilities

For the partnership to function properly, it is critical that both parties understand the division of roles and who owns what. First and foremost, the sales rep owns the account. They have ownership of the opportunity. At the end of the day, they ultimately have responsibility for the revenue. So, if there is any disagreement on how to approach an account or an opportunity, they hold the ultimate trump card. As the sales engineer, it's our job to get the technical win. This, of course, is a big part of closing the deal and winning the opportunity. As such, we are responsible for proposing the technical approach and suggest how we need to position the solution and demo to get the technical win. If there's a disagreement on how to approach the sale, it's our job to educate and inform the sales rep on what we believe to be the best approach. But at the end of the day, the sales rep *does* have the final say.

Establish and follow a process

We want to be agreeable, but we don't want to be doormats. We also don't want to be roadblocks. We want ample time to prepare but we don't want to waste time. We want to work well qualified opportunities but need to understand that sometimes they won't be. With so many competing objectives it is imperative that we establish a process with our sales counterparts and follow it.

Here is the list of touch points that you need to collaborate with your sales counterparts on and establish process for.

1. **Customer inquiry review**
    When a customer inquiry or request comes in, or a prospect agrees to a meeting that requires a demo, the first thing we need to do is review the customer situation BEFORE we schedule the presentation and demo.

2. **Technical discovery call**
    We will cover this in great depth in Chapter 3 but suffice it to say here that it is important to develop the habit of speaking with the customer yourself *before* you commit to a specific date for the meeting. Regardless of how well your sales counterpart may have qualified the opportunity, you are going to want to

hear with your own ears – directly from the prospect – their objectives, requirements, expectations, etc.

3. **Demo preparation**
   Be sure to negotiate enough time to prepare properly for the demonstration. This is covered in detail in Chapter 4.

4. **Logistics and planning**
   If the meeting requires on site access to the customer – be it local or long-distance travel – it requires planning and coordination. Make sure that this is part of the process. I've seen too many demos fail because logistics got messed up.

5. **Presentation and demo**
   Make sure that the demo you are planning to give aligns with the presentation that the sales rep is going to deliver.

6. **Post-demo issues, questions, and follow-up**
   If there are any follow up questions or issues to address, make sure to do so quickly.

7. **Post-demo discussion and lessons learned**
   Meet with the sales rep after the fact to discuss what worked, what didn't, what needs to be changed, etc. Sometimes this happens in the car on the way back to the airport. Sometimes this needs to be an explicitly scheduled in the following week.

8. **Product evaluation support**
   If there are any additional presales support items such as product evaluations or proofs of concept, make sure to provide appropriate support for those.

The diagram on the following page is a graphical representation of this process flow.

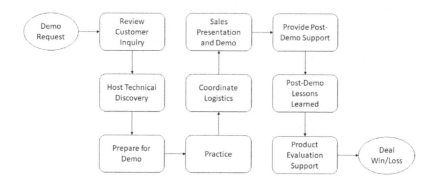

Figure 2: Example Presales Process

This is just an example of the process that you can develop and maintain between yourself and the sales reps you work with. Must you always follow it precisely? Of course not. Are there times that you may have to cut some corners, or make some exceptions in the interest of a sale? Yes. But by establishing this up front and agreeing to the fundamental way of doing business, you will develop a much stronger relationship with your sales counterparts and create an effective partnership – which is precisely the goal.

What if we disagree?

There will be times when there's a disagreement or a difference of opinion on how to approach a sales opportunity. I encourage you to work out agreements with your sales counterparts up front. As an example, they are not to agree to a demo with a customer until they've discussed it with you first. Until they've given you a chance to review the requirements and do some discovery of your own, they are not to commit to a date. In return, you will be as responsive and efficient as possible. At the end of the day, it's in everyone's best interest. One of the worst things that sales reps can do to is commit to a date for a customer demonstration that requires more prep time than has been budgeted for. It puts us under the gun and the deal at risk.

Customer Inquiry Review

When a customer requests a demo, or a prospect agrees to a meeting that requires a demo, the first thing you need to do is review the customer situation before you agree to a schedule. Use this list of questions to assess the opportunity.

1. Who are we talking to? What is their role/level?
2. Are they technical? Management? Executive level?
3. What are they trying to accomplish?
4. How long have we been talking to them?
5. Have they seen our product or a demonstration before?
6. Are they current customers?
7. Are they familiar with our product or have they seen or used a product like ours?
8. Is a third party or consultant involved?
9. In what stage is the opportunity?
10. Is there a budget and project tied to the opportunity?
11. Are we talking to the decision makers?
12. Are they on a timeline?

What are you doing here? You are doing your own due diligence. You're assessing the level of engagement so you can determine how much credence or priority you should place on this request. This is particularly important if you support multiple sales reps. If that is the case, you want to make sure that you are prioritizing those inquiries that are of highest value to you and the company. The goal is to work those opportunities in which we are engaged at the right level, tied to a budget, on a timeline, etc. Ideally you want to support "real opportunities" as opposed to scenarios in which the prospect is just "kicking the tires". Not that we never make time for "informational" demos that may lead to an opportunity down the road, but when you have competing requests and obligations, you want to be sure you are prioritizing correctly.

Schedule time for technical discovery

We will cover technical discovery in depth in the next chapter. However, in the context of Habit #1, it's important to establish as a foundational understanding between you and your sales reps that technical discovery is something you require. Establish, up front, that you expect to have the opportunity to host a technical discovery call *before* a meeting is scheduled. This is an important building block of an effective partnership, and it should be included as part of the sales cadence.

Budget time to prepare

Another important topic to discuss with your sales counterpart is allowing time for demo prep. As mentioned in the introduction, this is Habit #3 - to *prepare* for demos effectively and efficiently. We will cover that in depth in Chapter 4. However, suffice to say now that it, too, is an important aspect of building a good relationship with your sales counterparts. You deserve to have a say in how much time will be allowed for demo prep. It is incumbent upon you to be efficient and expedient. But the point here is to have the conversation in advance and set expectations appropriately, before you get into the heat of a deal.

Habit #1 Action Plan and Take-aways

Your sales counterpart is your PARTNER. The two of you are in this together. More than likely there will be fundamental differences between the two of you, but you *do* have a common goal – to win the deal. However, you both play different roles. Your job is to get the Technical Win. Their job is to close the deal. It requires collaboration, mutual respect, give and take. Neither one of you will be right all time. Neither one of you will be wrong all the time. Be proactive. Set expectations up front and talk through the issues.

Here's an action plan to develop this habit.

1. Get the right mindset – Sales is a Team Sport
2. Discuss and clarify roles and responsibilities – with your sales counterparts, sales management and fellow SEs
3. Map out a sales process – or review the sales process
4. Identify your responsibilities in each step of the process

CHAPTER 3

HABIT #2 - PROBE

The second habit may very well be the most important thing we can do to position ourselves to achieve the technical win. Habit #2 is to PROBE into the requirements of any request for a demo from a prospective client or customer. It is the habit of digging deeper into a customer's inquiry. What are their objectives? What are their requirements, constraints, expectations, previous experience, etc.? To do this effectively, we need to become masters at running, what I refer to as, the "Technical Discovery Call."

The Technical Discovery Call

The goal of the technical discovery call is to determine what it is that we need to say, show and do in order to get the technical win. Allow me to say that again for emphasis. The goal of the technical discovery call is to determine what it is that we need to SAY, SHOW and DO, in order to get the technical win.

In this chapter, we will first look at what the opposite is – what a sales engagement that does not include technical discovery looks like, and why that's an issue. We will discuss what it is that we should be probing for when we do get the opportunity. We'll review how to execute the discovery call effectively and what to expect. I will equip you with key techniques to skillfully navigate your way to success during these calls and provide you a list of sample questions you can use and customize to your specific needs.

Before we dive into that, let's consider the opposite. What does the absence of technical discovery look like? How does a sales opportunity that has not included a technical discovery call typically go?

What's the opposite?

The opposite of course is to work with the information we are provided, or none at all. If we don't follow the habit of probing into customer requests – of running technical discovery calls in advance of a product demo – it basically means we are going in blind to a sales meeting. We may have the information that our sales counterparts were able to extract and discover. And yes, we can present a standard, canned demonstration based on what he or she shared with us. We might even be able to create a semi-customized demo based on that information. But from my experience, as the person who is actually going to be standing in front of the customer, moving the mouse and talking through the demonstration, if I don't hear directly from the customer's mouth what it is they are trying to accomplish, what it is they are looking for, it leaves too much to chance.

What's the problem relying on the information from our sales counterpart?

There are numerous things. And no disrespect to the sales reps, but as we've established in an earlier chapter, they don't see the world the way we do. They are not the ones with fingers on the keyboard, and hands on the mouse. They are not the ones who will be challenged with difficult technical questions.

The more complex the software you sell and/or the bigger the deal and/or the more people involved in the purchase decision, the more important this is. What *sales reps* hear correlates to what they are trying to sell, how much they are hoping to sell, the sales strategy they plan to take, the people they need to engage with, etc. When we do discovery, what do *we* hear – or what *should* we be looking for? What we need to show, say and do – in relative specificity – in order to get the technical win. And, generally speaking, those two things – what they listen for and what we listen for – don't always align. Your sales counterpart is not going to ask the questions necessary to figure that out, at least, not likely.

You seem to be making a big deal of this

I can't emphasize the importance of the technical discovery call enough. In fact, most..., no, ALL the sales folks that I have worked with over the years have learned that this is a requirement of mine. They know not to just schedule demos without allowing time for technical discovery first. When they have a customer requesting a deep dive demo, the first thing they do is schedule me for a discovery call. This by the way builds upon Habit #1. If we don't have trust in the relationship, if the partnership isn't solid, then this may be a big ask. That's why it's so critically important to establish that partner mentality first.

Would this apply to everyone?

Allow me to set some context. I have sold complex software platforms into complex technical scenarios virtually my entire career. Many of the demos I've had to give require customization to be effective, and often times, significant customization. Under these circumstances, the technical discovery call is crucial. You may, however, sell a less complex platform. Your demonstrations may require less customization. As such, the technical discovery call may be less critical. I'm still of the opinion that even if you sell a more straightforward product, and even if your demos require less customization, it is still good practice to hold a discovery call. How else are you going to know exactly what to show and how to position it? Remember, you're the one under the spotlight with the mouse in your hand. Why wouldn't you want to talk to them once *before* you tout your wares?

What section of the newspaper do you read first?

Allow me to share an analogy. When you pick up the newspaper – for those of you who still read an actual printed newspaper – which section do you go to first? Which section does your spouse go to first? Or your parents? Or your kids?

I ask this question in my seminars. As you can imagine I get a wide range of responses. "*Sports! Fashion! Front page! Business! Travel!*" What's the point? Just like everyone picks up a newspaper and goes right to the section that they care about the most. You should start your demo with the section – or feature or capability – that your customer cares about most. Not what you like to show the most. Even if you sell a reasonably straightforward product that requires little customization, you still want to understand the perspective from which your audience is coming. What "section of the newspaper" are they most interested in? What portion or capability of your tool or software platform do they care about the most? Figure that out and lead with that in your demo.

In fact, that may be the only thing you need to show. How would you feel if you were forced to read the entire newspaper cover to cover, page by page, and had to wade through a bunch of uninteresting stories before you got to the one section you cared about? Why then would we put our audiences through the same agony? With the technical discovery call we can discover what they are most interested in and show them only that.

Sounds like you're speaking from experience

I can't tell you how many times – especially early in my career – I found myself mid-demo discovering, along the way, that our expectations – MY EXPECTATIONS – were completely wrong. I can't tell you how many times I found out, after it was too late, that the customer was looking for XYZ. Yet I was completely ill-prepared to show XYZ. Had I only known in advance, I could have prepared accordingly and hit the ball out of the park. (Sorry. That's another overused American phrase.) I could have prepared accordingly and done an exceptional job.

I HATE getting caught with my pants down. There were too many times that what the sales rep thought he or she heard was very different from what the prospective customer was actually looking for. I had no choice but to insist that I be given the opportunity to speak to the customer before I went on site to do the demo.

Once I started doing so, I discovered with alarming frequency, that what I heard was quite different from what the sales rep explained to me. Again, nothing against them. It's not their job to determine what needs to be demonstrated. That's MY job. That's OUR job. It's their job to close the deal and bring in the revenue. It's our job to get the technical win. But since it *is* our job, we need to take ownership of those requirements.

He/she who buys a shovel...

Anyone who's attended one of my seminars has heard me share this. It's one of my favorites. And it applies here.

He/she who buys a shovel doesn't want a shovel. They want a hole. But they don't just want a hole, they want a fence or a tree. But they don't just want a fence or a tree, they want privacy, or shad, or fruit, or flowers. Yet we show up wanting to talk about the shiny shovel!

Why do we run the technical discovery call? Because by in large, if we sell software, it's equivalent to the shovel – it's a tool for getting things done. And just like "he who buys a shovel," he (or she) who buys software typically doesn't want software. They want to do something with the software. Our challenge is to figure out what it is that they are trying to accomplish with a software solution, and then demonstrate for them how they can accomplish that with OUR software.

What do we *know, not know and need to know*?

Please consider this. What is it that we inherently *know*? We know what our products are capable of. We know (at least we should know) what our unique value proposition is and what our key selling points are. We know what our best use cases are, what our most compelling features and capabilities are. We know how to best position and demonstrate our products. (At least we should.) That's what we're hired to do. And more than likely, that's the sort of training you got when you joined the company, and probably the sort of training you get on a regular basis at the annual kickoff. Simply put, we know ourselves, our company and our product.

What do we *not* know? We don't know the unique perspective from which our customer is coming. We don't (necessarily) know their business, their project team, their culture, their dynamics, their objectives, their unique requirements, etc. I could go on and on here, but I'm sure you get the point. We don't know what we don't know. We can guess. We have a hunch based on the simple fact that they are considering our software. That certainly narrows the playing field. But at the end of the day, we don't really know what it is that they are trying to accomplish, and all the context around it.

What do we *need* to know? Well, just that. We need to understand their unique situation. We need to gather as much information about the team, the organization, the project, etc. so that we can map our capabilities and solutions to their needs and requirements.

That's what this technical discovery call is all about. It's a mapping exercise. We know what we'd like to show. We know the features, functions, and capabilities that usually impress our customers. We know why organizations typically purchase our software. But rather than just going in to "show up and throw up", we want to tie everything we want them to see, with the specific problems they are trying to solve – the specific things they are trying to accomplish. So how do we do this?

What are we probing for?

What information should we be trying to dig up in the context of the technical discovery call? The following is a list of things you should be looking for when you run the technical discovery call.

1. Goals/Objectives – at the end of the day, what are they trying to accomplish? What's the mission?
2. Motivation – what is their motivation? Is there or was there a compelling event? Is there a change of leadership? Change in the business? Or are they just tired of dealing with X or not being able to do Y? Is the project related to an overarching corporate strategy or objective?
3. Burning Issues – what are the burning issues that are keeping people up at night, causing people to lose jobs, costing them money, wasting time, losing business, etc.
4. Success – what does success look like for them? Have they considered that? Do they even know? And how will they measure success? What KPIs are they using?
5. Requirements – do they have specific requirements they are trying to address? Specific constraints they need to work within? Are they governed by specific regulations, legislation, policy, etc.?
6. Capabilities – are there specific capabilities they are looking for? Do they currently have any home-grown solutions that they want to mimic?

7. History – what is their history with your company or product? Do they have any history with other products or companies in the space? Have they attempted this and failed? Why?
8. Context – is there any other contextual information that will help prepare for the meeting? Are there competing opinions within the group? Are there multiple groups with different agendas?
9. Participants – who will be in the room? What are their roles? Are they familiar with solutions like these? Are they part of the decision-making team?
10. Logistics – what are the logistics? How large is the room? Is it a secure environment? Will I have internet access? What are the AV equipment options?

Expect some pushback

Despite how important and critical we think the technical discovery call is, you may very well get some pushback – at least at first – from your sales counterparts. The biggest argument I hear is that in their mind they've already qualified the opportunity. They've already given you the information that you need to go off and build a demo and prepare for the demonstration. They might even just want you to show up and give the standard canned demo.

Furthermore, they may be reluctant to get the customer on yet another phone call. They may worry that the customer will feel like they're being badgered, or they're being asked to provide information or answer questions that they've already been asked. That in some way, another discovery call would make the sales team look bad. And frankly, it's a legitimate argument. We don't want the customer to feel like they're being badgered. We don't want the customer to feel like they're being asked to provide information that's already been provided. So how do we handle this?

Do your homework

There are a couple of very specific things we need to do to mitigate the pushback. First, we need to do our homework. We need to capture and collect whatever information we can from our sales counterparts. What *do* we already know? What has the customer already shared. (Again, this is another example of the importance of having a good partnership with our sales colleagues to ensure there is effective communication between us.)

Then once you're armed with all the information your colleague has gathered to date, you're going to use that as part of the discovery call. Keep in mind you want to be as efficient with the prospect's time as you possibly can. Try to keep the technical discovery call to about 30 minutes.

INSIGHT: I've had to say this countless times to the sales folks that I work with, and I'll share with you now. If a prospect isn't willing to spend 30 minutes on the phone with the technical expert who's going to give the demonstration – to clarify the requirements and expectations. Then there's no way on earth that that customer is going to spend any money on your solution. Period. To me, it's an indication of how serious – or NOT – a prospective client really is.

Execute the call

When you do get on the phone with the customer – typically with your sales counterpart. Thank them for their time, and then say something like the following:

> *"<Mr. or Mrs. Customer>, my colleague Mike has given me some background on the project, and I understand you're looking to accomplish XYZ. Since I will be the one on site to present our solution to you, I'd like to take just a few minutes of your time to ask you a few more questions to make sure that I fully understand what it is that you're*

looking for from a technical perspective. That way, when we are on site for the demonstration, it will be the best use of your time. "Is that an agreeable approach for you?"

Then once you have permission to proceed, so to speak, start by asking a very open-ended question. Your opening should sound something like, *"I understand from Mike that you are trying to do XYZ. Could you, in your own words, give me a 30- or 60- second overview of the project just to make sure we're on the same page?"* Almost invariably, the prospect or customer you're speaking to will take five to ten minutes (or more) answering that first question. Why? What do people like talking about the most? Themselves! And their work or their projects. Just opening the door with that one question allows for the prospect to elaborate on what they are trying to do.

OK, I started the call. What next?

While the customer is answering your first question, what should you be doing? Frantically taking notes, paying VERY close attention to what it is they're saying. And what is it that you're looking for? Points, concepts, issues, objectives, etc. to drill down further on.

In that first five or ten minutes, you should be able to start imagining what it is that you need to demonstrate to align your solution with their project objectives and requirements. As you hear certain key words that correlate to capabilities or solutions that you might want to show, we are going to drill into those further with probing questions. Remember, this process will ultimately dictate what you show during the meeting. The goal of the technical discovery call is for us to walk away with a very clear idea in our mind of what it is that we're going to SAY, SHOW, and DO in the context of the demo.

After they have responded to your initial question, and you have frantically jotted down some key points, words and phrases, what you do next is critical to the success of the technical discovery call.

The very next question needs to relate to something they said during their brief overview. It should go something like this: *"You mentioned something about digital transformation. Can you elaborate on exactly what that means in your organization?"* Or you might say, *"It sounds like you are trying to better align your IT organization with your functional business units. Did I understand that correctly and have you attempted to do something like this in the past?"*

This sounds important

It is! You're doing a couple of things here. First, you're demonstrating that you were actually paying attention to the answer. Second, you're showing sincere interest and curiosity for what it is that they are trying to do. And third, you're also gathering additional information that will help you give an even better, more focused demo.

This is important for a couple of reasons. More than likely the person you are talking to has a key role in the purchase decision, so you are beginning to develop rapport with this individual. The second, and arguably more importantly, it is necessary to keep the flow of the discovery call going.

What's the reverse? I've seen sales engineers get on a discovery call. They ask the overarching question, listen to the response, and then ask a follow-on question which is completely unrelated to what the prospect has just shared with them. This is such a big mistake. It gives the impression that they were not paying any attention to the response, and frankly, that they just don't care.

To illustrate this point – how to start with a key question and then follow it with more probing questions – see the graphic on the next page. The first figure represents an effective Q&A session, in which each question spawns from something the customer said. It represents the ideal flow of a discovery call. The second figure represents an ineffective flow. This second example is a bit like "badgering the witness."

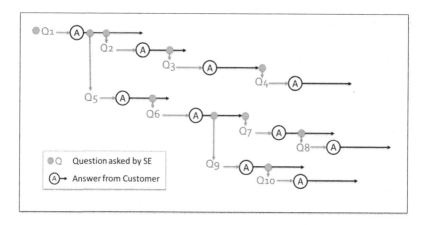

Figure 3: An effective Q&A flow during technical discovery

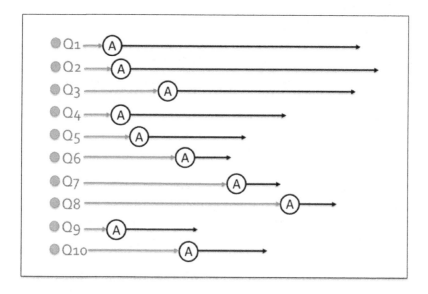

Figure 4: Ineffective Q&A flow during technical discovery

INSIGHT: *No matter where the prospect goes with his/her answer to the first question, your next question needs to correlate to something they said in their answer.*

So, ask your second question. One that directly relates to something they said in their opening response and ideally something that relates to a core capability in your software. In other words, let's also move a step closer to your objective which is to determine what and how you need to present your solution in order to get the technical win. Then continue down this path – asking questions that correlate to their responses, probing deeper and deeper into their requirements, and objectives.

What if they don't give me anything to work with?

Good question. I have a couple of thoughts. First, if you're that far off base then have a conversation with your sales counterpart. Leads may not be getting adequate qualification, so discuss the kind of questions that are being asked before an opportunity hits your radar. If a reasonable amount of qualification is being done up front, you shouldn't find yourself on a discovery call where there's a total mismatch between their objectives and your solution. Second, sometimes some of the prospects we speak with do have a hard time articulating their goals and objectives. Sometimes it does take some probing, and some patience to drill down into what it is that they are truly looking for. So, I maintain, find something that they said that you can leverage or integrate into your next question and go from there.

How long do we keep this up?

Another good question! Any one of these "threads" (i.e., series of related questions and responses), is typically going to end in one of three places – typically after about 3-5 questions in succession.

1. You will arrive at a specific requirement that you can address in your demo and now have the information you need to do so effectively. This clearly is the ideal case and what we are ultimately striving for. If you do land there, that particular thread should end something like this:

   You: *"It sounds like you are trying to accomplish ABC, given (fill in the blank) constraints, within (fill in the blank) parameters, without having to do XYZ. Does it sound like I have that basically correct?"*

   Prospect: *"Yes. That's actually very good. That's precisely what we're trying to do."*

   You: *"Great. For what it's worth, we see this a lot. In fact, many of our customers are trying to do or have done similar things to what we're talking about here. I'm quite confident that you will be very satisfied with what you are going to see next week. I'm excited to show you what's possible with our solution."*

2. They may redirect onto another more specific, more important topic. In other words, your prospect starts down one path, but as you probe deeper, you discover that what they really are looking for is something very different. We're sort of back up to the top starting a new thread – a new series of questions and answers, until we arrive at one of the other end points, or another redirect.

3. The third scenario – and this is the one we least want to discover, but still better to discover now than later – is we get to a point where we can adequately articulate what it is that they are trying to do and accomplish, but it is NOT well suited for our solution. That is, we discover that our software may not be a particularly good fit for their requirements or objectives. When this happens, and it WILL happen, I encourage you not to "show your hand," so to speak, right then and there. Continue and complete the discovery call, and then discuss the issue with

your sales counterpart after the call. There is no need to deal with that issue then and there. That particular thread may end something like this:

You: *"It sounds like you are trying to accomplish ABC, given (fill in the blank) constraints, within (fill in the blank) parameters, without having to do XYZ. Does it sound like I have that basically correct?"*

Prospect: *"Yes. That's actually very good. That's precisely what we're trying to do."*

You: *"And just to be clear, this is a critical part of what you are trying to do, yes? This is a must have, if you will."*

Prospect: *"Yeah. This is really important. If we can't address this most everything else is irrelevant."*

You: *"OK. Good to know. I have a couple thoughts on how we will address this next week. But I will discuss with Bob the best way to approach this, and we'll go from there."*

And then continue with the discovery call. The issue you've just uncovered may or may not be a showstopper, but you still want to collect as much information as possible. Who knows, they may think that's the one thing they're looking for, but you may discover that there are other items that you can address, that they weren't even aware of. There's almost always a way in, you just need to be patient and collect as much information as possible.

How do we know when we're done?

Let's go back to the goal of the technical discovery call. It's to determine, to the best of our ability, in as little time as possible, what it is that we need to say, show, and do when we get on site (or online) to get the technical win. So how do we know when we're done? When we have formulated in our mind a good idea of what it

73

is that we going to show. After 20 or 30 minutes of discovery, we should have a pretty good idea of the capabilities we need to highlight. We should have a good sense for who's going to be in the room. We should have a sense for how much customization is going to be involved. And we should have a rough outline – in our minds, if not on paper, of what it is that we are going to present.

What if I can't get there in 30 minutes?

It's a valid question. And it does take some practice. But I challenge you. Typically, a demo is going to run anywhere from 20-45 minutes, depending on the complexity of the technology you are selling. If it takes longer to demonstrate then (in my opinion) there's an issue with the demonstration strategy and approach – we'll cover that in later chapter. For now, let's assume that your demo will be no longer than 20-40 minutes. And during that time, you should only be covering 3-5 key points or key capabilities of the software. Anything more, and it tends to be too much anyways. (Again, this is something else we will cover at length later in the book.) Given that we are trying to identify 3-5 key points to make during the demo, I have a hard time believing that, if we are being efficient with time during the call and effective with our questions, that we cannot come up with a demo plan in 30 minutes or less. Particularly given that our sales rep has already provided some background and context. If you find that you cannot sort out what you need to demonstrate in that amount of time, I encourage you to work on the effectiveness of your questions, narrow the focus, and work to drive the conversation with a little more assertiveness.

Our Biggest Mistake

I hope by now you are completely convinced that technical discover is something you should be doing with most every deal – depending of course on the size, complexity, strategic value, etc. However, before you jump into the game of running these technical discovery calls, allow me to share with you the biggest mistake that I see SEs make during these conversations.

The biggest mistake that SEs make when running one of these calls is the moment they hear something that their software addresses – an objective, a requirement, a burning issue, etc. – they jump into "sell and tell mode", and forget all about the purpose of the meeting – discovery through asking questions. They latch on to one key point and start telling the prospect all about how their solution does this, and that. *"We can solve it this way and we can solve it that way."* This is a big mistake and frankly, a lost opportunity.

During the technical discovery call, now is NOT the time to sell. Now is NOT the time to solve. Now is the time to ASK QUESTIONS. Probe deeper into their responses. And collect the information you need to create the most compelling, engaging, spot-on demo as possible. Period. In as nice a way as I can say it. Ask good questions. And then shut up and listen! Remember, it typically takes four or five rounds of questions to get to the heart of what it is they are trying to accomplish.

The time to sell is coming. That's why you're going onsite to do a demo. The time to solve is coming. That's what your post-sales consultants are responsible for. Remember, your goal is to get the technical win. And the goal of this technical discovery call is to collect as much information as you can to create the best demo possible. The more you talk during this call, the less information you are collecting.

Take the trip

Aslan Training, a sales training organization based in Atlanta, Georgia has a great term for this. They call it 'Take the Trip.' Imagine a picture of the globe. You are standing at the North Pole and your prospect is standing at the South Pole. When we begin the technical discovery call, I want you to imagine that you are on polar opposite positions with your prospect. With every question, you take a step closer to their side of the globe. If at any point, you stop to sell or stop to solve, until you have "taken the trip" all the way around the globe – meaning all the way around until you fully see the problem, the situation, the objective from their point of view, you are selling yourself – and your customer, short. During the technical discovery call, be sure to take the full trip around to their point of view, and then tie it back to the specific things you need to SAY, SHOW, and DO during the demo to get the technical win.

Sample Questions

If hosting technical discovery calls is not something you have done before, you may not know where to start. Here is a list of questions to help get you started. Use this set of questions to help drive the technical discovery call. Use these verbatim or modify to suit your particular selling situations.

1. Could I trouble you to provide me with an overview of the project in your own words?
2. Is it possible to provide some background as to why you're looking at tools such as ours?
3. Does the organization have any previous experience with other tools or solutions like ours? If so, how did it go? If it failed, why?
4. At the end of the day, what are you hoping to accomplish with this solution or with this project?
5. What does success look like for your organization?
6. Are there specific industry standards, frameworks, or guidelines that you are required to do or attempting to follow? Are you even familiar with them and are they important to you?
7. Are there certain business areas, domains, or internal organizations that you are targeting or focusing on to begin with?
8. Will the business context of the demonstration make a difference to you and your group? (As an example, if they are an insurance agency, will a demonstration that includes sample data from a fictitious manufacturing company make it difficult for them to follow?)

9. If so, do they have any sample data that they could provide to be included in the demonstration?
10. Are there specific capabilities that you're looking for?
11. Who's going to be in attendance? What are their roles? Are they hand-on users, technical principals, management, decision makers, etc.?
12. What are the meeting logistics? Is it a secure environment? Will I have internet access? Are we meeting in a conference room or someone's office?

Ask in their context, not yours

Allow me to clarify an important point here. The questions we ask need to be in the context of your customer's perspective – not yours. Let me explain. At the end of the day, what do we care about the most, as it pertains to this conversation? Figuring out what features, functions and capabilities of the software we need to demonstrate to get the technical win. That is our objective with this technical discovery call. But what do the people we are speaking with care about? Their objectives. Their project. Their issues. Their requirements. Etc. Thus, all of our questions need to be asked in the context of what THEY are trying to accomplish, what THEIR objectives are, what THEIR requirements are, etc. It is then our job to interpret and translate what they are saying into what it means in the context of our products.

Another mistake I've seen SEs make when trying to run a technical discovery call is, they ask questions in the context of their tool or from their vantage point, not that of their customer. I've quite literally heard sales engineers open with *"So what are the features or capabilities of our tool that you'd like to see?"* NO! "Which of our use cases do you think you fit into?" NO! "Which of our tools would you like me to show you?" NO! NO! NO! This is not technical discovery. This is basically asking the prospect to do your job for you. They have no idea what features they want you to show them. They're looking to you as the expert to show them how your solution satisfies their requirements. Please, please, please ask your questions in the context of your customers point of view, not yours. (OK. I'm off my soapbox now.)

What if I'm dealing with some savvy prospects?

You may be dealing with some prospects who have used tools like yours in the past, or maybe even yours. If that's the case, they may know EXACTLY what they want to see. They may know exactly what they want you to show the other members of the team. I'm quite certain that will come out during the call. There's no need to ask for that directly. If in the unlikely event you do get a prospect who is that precise and prescriptive about what it is that they are looking for, consider it a gift and roll with it. But don't approach the conversation that way. In most cases, it's a pathway to failure.

Leading the Witness

Another important technique worth noting is what I refer to as 'Leading the Witness.' We all have features or capabilities in the software we sell that we LOVE to demonstrate. I'm quite certain you know what I'm talking about. The "bells and whistles," as we like to say, that get the "Ooohs and Aaahhs." In fact, they are often referred to as 'demo features' or sales features. They're the visuals, or functions that show well and differentiate our products from the competition.

Whenever you run a technical discovery call, you should always have those key features on the back of your mind and keep an eye open (or an ear open to be precise) for any opportunity to position one of these key features. In fact, when you hear the prospect mention something that relates to one of these key features, be sure to explicitly drill in on that point to draw out more information. The more closely you can align the strengths of your software to the items that are important to them, the better the demo is going to be.

What happens if we are nearing the end of the technical discovery call – we've collected about all the information we need, we have a good understanding of what it is they are looking for, what it is they are trying to do – and they haven't said anything that ties to the best thing we have to show them? Does that mean we're going to leave our 'sexiest feature' out of the demo? Not necessarily. This is where I would be inclined to *lead the witness*. I might say, *"You know, before we end the call, there is one other thing that I wanted to ask. A lot of the folks that we are working with look for XYZ in a platform like ours. That topic hasn't come up, so I'm just wondering if that's something you've considered. Might you be interested in seeing something like that?"*

What are we doing here? We're planting a seed. Yes, we're leading the witness. Maybe it's something they hadn't even considered. Maybe it's something they didn't know was possible. Maybe it's something he wanted to see but forgot to mention. And maybe it's none of the above. Maybe it is something they're aware of but it's just not something they're too concerned about. Whatever the case may be, we want to know now – is this something we should show them or not? Particularly if this is something we almost always include in our demonstrations, because it shows so well. If it hasn't come up during the context of the technical discovery call, we want to know if there's a reason to show it, or, more importantly, a good reason not to.

Who's going to be in the room?

Once you have identified the key objectives, requirements, etc. and tied it to the specific features, functions, capabilities that you are going to show, it's important to cover a few non-technical items before you end the call. We need to understand who's going to be in the room. Is the audience highly technical in nature? Will it be the people who will be using the software? Will it be management and/or the decision makers? Are there key players in the room that have a stronger voice in the decision-making process? Are all the participants on the same team or will different groups be represented in the room? Will they have the same objectives and agenda as the person with whom you're speaking?

The answer to the questions above will further dictate how you prepare for the meeting. If it's going to be a largely technical crowd, then you can be prepared to go reasonably deep with some of your explanations. If it's a higher-level meeting with management and executives, then your message and demonstration need to be higher level and emphasize the business case and value proposition. If it's a large group, they will be less likely to ask questions and engage, so you probably need to be prepared for it to be more one directional – i.e., you talking to them. If it's going to be a smaller, more intimate group, then you can be prepared to be more collaborative, and conversational. All these finer details help ensure a smooth, and successful demo.

INSIGHT: *I've used the terms "features and functions" a number of times in this chapter. Allow me to say that when it comes time to preparing for the demo – which is Habit #3, covered in depth in the next chapter – we are NOT going to do a "features and functions" demo. We are going to create a script for the demo and tell a story. We will weave the key features and functions that we want to demonstrate into that story. So please do not be alarmed by the fact that I'm using the words features and functions here. At this point in the process, it is important to identify the specific things that we need to demonstrate. But in the next step, we are going to discuss how to weave all these items together into a cohesive, compelling, meaningful story. So, stay tuned for that.*

In addition to who's going to be in the room, ask about the room itself. Why? Because the physical nature and proximity of the room can impact the flow of the demo. I remember going in to do a demo once and knew that we were meeting with one guy – one key technical principle. It was me and my sales counterpart. I was prepared to make the session very interactive, very collaborative. When we got there, he took us down to a large auditorium. He put me on stage, and he sat in the front row. (Seriously. I can't make this up folks.) It was one of the most awkward, uncomfortable demonstrations I have ever given. There I was expecting this intimate, collaborative conversation-style 'demonstration.' And there he was sitting back expecting a seminar style presentation. I was completely and totally unprepared for that.

The reverse has also been true. I've gone into demonstrations thinking we would have a nice conference room with video and room to maneuver and found myself demonstrating from my laptop in someone's cube on their desk with a handful of people huddled around the monitor. Again, it threw me off my game. I handled it, but it was a challenge. And, as I mentioned before, I hate being caught off guard. (Actually, I think I said I hate being caught with my pants down. Suffice it to say that I hate both.)

What's the point? These may seem like minor details. They may seem trivial. But if you have hundreds of thousands of dollars or even million-dollar deals on the line, nothing is trivial. You are going to want to know as much as you can about what you're going to encounter before you get on site to do the demo.

Incidentally, I realize that I frequently mention "going on site" to do the demo. I recognize that many demonstrations are done over the web now. So obviously, if it's a web demonstration, the size of the room matters not. And when I say "go on site" clearly, I'm also referring to web demonstrations as well. Most of what we are talking about with regards to the technical discovery call applies equally to a demo in person and a demo over the web. In fact, it may even be more important for the very fact that you are not in the room and cannot read body language or other nonverbal communication cues. More on that topic to come.

What if there isn't time for Technical Discovery?

This is something I hear quite frequently. And frankly, something that I encounter from time to time. So, what do we do if we don't have the opportunity to run a technical discovery call before the demo? What then?

First, let's consider the circumstances under which this typically happens. It might be the result of our sales counterpart just dropping the ball. They forget to schedule the call. Or they get lazy or they don't believe in, or agree with, the importance of the technical discovery call. If that's the case, we need to go back to Habit #1 and work on the partnership a little bit to improve our presales cadence.

For the moment, however, let's assume that's not the case. Let's assume you have a good working relationship with your sales counterpart, and that there are extenuating circumstances around a particular opportunity. Maybe they have a budget that must be used by a certain date and they are coming up on the deadline. Maybe they've been waiting to get access to a key person who is difficult to get time with, and they finally managed to get time – tomorrow. Whatever the case may be, let's assume that the salesperson is operating in good faith, as is the prospect, and there just isn't time for a technical discovery call.

Clearly, we don't want to say no to the invitation for a meeting. Remember, we don't want to be roadblocks. We don't want to be revenue impediments. So, I encourage you to agree to do the demo but, make it clear upfront that without the opportunity to do any discovery of your own, the best you can do is a "canned demo", and that you would like to begin with some discovery in real time, to make sure you highlight those capabilities, or features that are most in line with what they are looking for.

Allow me to give you an example. I recently got a phone call from one of my sales reps on a Thursday afternoon. He said "Chris, I really need you to do a demo tomorrow morning for me." (Friday morning!) What was worse, he couldn't even be on a call! He explained that they've been working this deal for a while. It's a 'hot opportunity' and they're suddenly in a position where they've got some budget they can use, but it's got to be acted on quickly. The last step was for the key technical principle to see a couple of key things so that he could endorse the purchase and move forward. My colleague had just received the news that day, was already scheduled to be on site with another customer the next day and couldn't escape that commitment.

Let me set some additional context. The sales rep that made this request is someone that I've worked with for years. He and I had a very good working relationship. As you can imagine, my first response was, *"Well you know (name withheld to protect the innocent), I don't do demos without doing discovery calls up front. But for YOU, I'll do it."* Then I went on to explain that I had no choice but to use a standard, canned demonstration that I had previously prepared which he understood. I further explained that I would open the meeting by doing a little bit of discovery up front, and that I would do my best to pivot and shift on the fly.

The next day we got on the call – it was a demonstration over the web, just this one technical principle and me. I opened the meeting the way I would a technical discovery call. I said,

> *"This is what my colleague explained to me about your project and what you're looking to accomplish. I understand the situation and I've got a demonstration ready to go. It's one of our standards, canned software demonstrations. But before I get started, could I trouble you to take 30 to 60 seconds to tell me a little bit more about the project, in your own words, so that I can have a little more context for the demonstration?"*

Without missing a beat, he spent about 10 minutes telling me about the project, the history of what they've been trying to do, their biggest issues, what they're ultimately trying to accomplish, etc., etc. I asked a few questions along the way, and he went a little bit deeper on a couple of key points. About 12 minutes into that conversation I had an ah-ha moment. I got a clear picture in my mind of exactly what he needed to see to make his endorsement and get the deal done. With that, I aborted the standard demo I was going to give. I brought up one screen, and we talked through a few key capabilities that aligned with the pain points he had just been describing.

He was completely, and totally engaged. Completely and totally enthralled with the solution I was presenting. And later that day, my sales colleague was informed that they were moving forward with the purchase. I had successfully achieved the technical win, and that proved to be the tipping point on closing the deal. As it turned out, it ended up being the biggest sale of the quarter and one of the largest deals of the year.

What's the point here? Will you always have the opportunity to host a technical discovery call in advance of the live demonstration? No, you won't. Is it ideal if you can? Yes, I believe it is. But unfortunately, we don't live in a perfect world and things don't always go to plan. However, if you do find yourself in a sales situation in which hosting a technical discovery call is simply not an option, you can still do some technical discovery in real time. My advice is be prepared to show something compelling, but also be prepared to pivot and turn on a dime. Do some discovery at the very beginning of your demo. If you discover that one thing that will make the sale, but it isn't part of your canned demo. Abort, switch gears, and show them what they really care about.

Selling a concept vs. a product

Another thing to listen for when hosting the technical discovery call is whether you are selling a concept vs. positioning your product. What do I mean by this? Most software products exist within a given category or industry domain. For example, SalesForce.com is CRM, Symantec is the "leader in cyber security" (it says so on their website), Documentum is enterprise content management, etc. These categories are fairly well known. If you're selling a well-known product in a well-known category like these, it's highly unlikely the people you will be presenting to will need to be sold on the idea of having a CRM or strengthening their cyber security posture.

However, in this ever-changing, ever-evolving world of information, technology and innovation, you may very well find yourself selling a product that doesn't fit neatly into a well-known category. You may be selling a product in a brand new or emerging category. For over a decade, I sold software in the Enterprise Architecture domain. It has now become a fairly well know category, but in the early days, there was a great deal of confusion about what Enterprise Architecture was. There was a great deal of skepticism with regards to its value to the organization. I regularly faced situations in which I had to sell the idea of Enterprise Architecture and its value proposition FIRST, before I could say a word about what made our solution unique and special. Without selling the idea or concept first, there was little point in pitching our software.

If you find yourself in this situation, there is an important distinction that you need to make during the discovery call. Are you going to be presenting to people who are well versed in your domain or category? Have they already bought in to the idea that this is something they need? If so, then the challenge at hand is to demonstrate the unique benefits of working with your software, and your company. If they have not, you may very well need to start out by selling the concept behind the category and help them justify the investment to begin with.

This became crystal clear to me one day as I was launching into a presentation and demonstration for a Federal Government prospect. They had come into our office for a demonstration of our enterprise architecture platform. I began the session with a handful of slides that I commonly used to establish the importance of enterprise architecture, the value to organizations, why it was important to the Federal Government, etc. After the first slide, the manager of the group could tell where this was going. She quite literally stopped mid-sentence and said, *"Chris. Let me stop you* right there. We don't need a pitch on Enterprise Architecture. We get it. We've bought in. We're drinking the Kool-Aid. We just need to understand why we should select your solution over your competitors." With that I rapidly shifted gears and went into the product demonstration. She made it perfectly clear where they were and what they were looking for. But from that moment on, whenever I hosted a technical discovery call, I knew to listen for this very thing. Where was this group? Had they already bought into the idea of what we are selling? Have they already made the decision to do something? Is my competition the other vendors in our space? Or is my competition the status quo? This can be an incredibly important distinction.

Selling TO vs. Selling WITH

The final thought that I'll leave you with on this topic of the technical discovery call is to identify whether you are selling TO the person that you are speaking with or selling WITH them. Allow me to explain. Presumably, the person with whom you have the technical discovery call is the individual who has been selected to represent the interests of the decision-making team. Given the nature of the call, this person is more than likely technical in nature. Maybe they are one of the technical principles on the team. Maybe they will be one of the primary users. Sometimes they might be someone in a management role. Whatever the case, for argument sake we will call them your technical sponsor – which is to say that they are the individual providing some technical insight and guidance.

One of the things that I look for during the discovery call is where is this person coming from in terms of their position or perception of our solution? Have they used us before? Are they familiar with our software? Are they advocates? Quite often the person you are dealing with on the discovery call may have previous experience with your software; they're familiar with what it can do, and they are on a crusade to bring you into the organization. If this is the case, you're really not selling *to* them, you're selling *with* them. This turns the technical discovery call into a very different conversation. We can now plan and collaborate on how best to position the capabilities of the tool together. We no longer have to sell them on the capabilities of the tool. Quite the contrary, we can use them as our coach to help us figure out how to sell to their colleagues, and vice versa.

The reason I bring this to your attention is that I've witnessed – on numerous occasions – technical discovery calls hosted by people who have worked with and for me, who didn't pick up on this nuance. Or if they did, they didn't use it to their advantage. The mistake I see people make is they maintain a "sell to" stance even after they've discovered that their technical sponsor is actually a "friendly" – someone that they can safely confide in and collaborate with. I've also seen the reverse. I've seen sales engineers assume the technical sponsor was in their corner, to find out later it wasn't necessarily the case. Just because they are working with you as the technical point of contact, does not necessarily mean that they are in your camp. You may still have a sales job to do on them. So, look for this. Be tuned in to this subtlety and know when to lock arms and sell together.

Free Gift...

To help you develop the skills of effective discovery and better manage a discovery conversation, I invite you to download a Technical Discovery Worksheet at the following link:

www.demodoctor.com/discoveryworksheet

Habit #2 Action Plan and Take-aways

Technical discovery is different from traditional sales qualification and discovery. We see and hear things different than our sales counterparts. Our goal is to determine what we need to SAY, SHOW, and DO – in the context of the demo – in order to get the technical win. The opposite is to go in blind. Or go into the demo with only the information provided by our sales counterpart, which may or may not be enough for us to give a compelling demo.

Every customer, opportunity and/or situation is unique. We need to lead with and demonstrate those capabilities that will mean the most to our audience, not to us. Remember the concept of the newspaper. What section of the newspaper would you read first? Discover the answer to this question for your prospect. Do this by asking good questions, that spawn from their responses. Be conversational. Don't badger the witness. Be effective and efficient with their time. And please remember to just LISTEN! And take good notes. Now is NOT the time to sell. Now is NOT the time to solve. Formulate a plan and save it for the demo.

Action plan to develop this habit:

1. Discuss the approach with your sales counterpart
2. Budget time for technical discovery
3. Do your homework
4. Prepare a list of questions in advance
5. Ask questions that flow conversationally
6. Follow the prospect or customer wherever they go and ask questions accordingly
7. *Lead the witness* when appropriate
8. LISTEN, LISTEN, LISTEN

CHAPTER 4

HABIT #3 - PREPARE

Habit #3 is to PREPARE for demonstrations with both effectiveness, and efficiency in mind. Mastering this habit will pay dividends in job satisfaction, as it will improve your productivity, give hours, days and weeks of your life back to you, and increase your personal income. It will endear you to your sales counterparts, because you won't delay deals in the pipeline. It will also delight your customers because your demonstrations will be tailor-made to their interests, objectives and requirements. They won't be bored to death by demos that either don't make sense to them or don't apply to them.

Allow me to emphasize a key point here right up front. At face value, Habit #3 may seem obvious. You might be thinking to yourself, *"Prepare? That's Habit #3? Of course, we should prepare."*

In this chapter, we're not only going to talk about the importance of preparation, how best to do it, and what to focus on. We are going to talk about preparing in such a manner that you don't delay deals and/or risk burnout yourself. What we're really talking about is how to create compelling customized demos – that explicitly address your prospective customers' unique needs – in the most efficient and expedient manner. What separates the highest performing sales engineers from the rest is not just that they prepare, it's the way in which they prepare and what they focus on that makes the difference.

One of the most important themes of this chapter is understanding the difference between developing *demo content* vs. the *demo script*. Demo content is WHAT we are going to show. The demo script is what we are going to SAY, how we are going to say it, and the order in which we are going to say it. Incidentally, you can also think of this as the story you are going to tell as you flow through the demo. As engineers, we tend to focus on the content – what it is we are building – and not the story. And yet, the story is invariably more important than what we show. Without a story, and without context for how the demonstration the audience is being presented aligns with their objectives, it almost doesn't matter what we build; it's going to fall flat. However, with context, and a compelling story, the content that we build comes alive in the eyes of the audience. Problem is, when many of us prepare for a demo, the 'thing' we are building gets the lion's share of our attention and the story becomes an afterthought. That's precisely what we are going to address in this chapter.

Another key theme of this chapter is focus. Our focus naturally tends to gravitate to ourselves – our product, our solution, the features, and functions (aka "bells and whistles") of our tool. The most effective sales engineers shift their focus to the customer – their objectives, their requirements, etc. Why? Our goal is to get the technical win. Our goal is to get our prospects to say yes. How can we possibly expect to do so if we are not demonstrating capabilities in the context of what they care about? So, we are going to shift our mindset from what WE like to and want to demonstrate to what THEY ultimately need to see and hear to say yes. It's in their best interest, and it's in ours as well.

Common Mistakes

There are three mistakes that we see most often in the field:

1. We UNDERPREPARE (or we don't prepare at all)
2. We OVERPREPARE – which wastes time and sets us up for problems during the demo
3. We focus too much on CONTENT and too little on SCRIPT

Let's consider each one of these in more detail.

Underpreparing

If Habit #3 is to prepare, what's the opposite? To not prepare at all – or to prepare very, very little. When that is the case, more than likely it means that we are using a pre-canned demo, i.e. a standard demo that was previously created, with a common set of data and a standard script – typically used for training and very basic, introductory demonstrations. Sometimes this is referred to as "show up and throw up." As a result, we tend to treat every customer, every opportunity, and/or every situation the same.

Why is This a Problem?

For starters, the focus is all on us – our product, our solution, our expertise, etc. It assumes all prospects have the same problems, the same issues, objectives, etc. We run the risk of boring our audience – likely showing them things they don't care about or understand. As a result of not preparing properly, we might miss or overlook things they do care about. There are numerous reasons why this is not the most effective approach.

Allow me to offer the other side of the coin. There are benefits to using a canned, predefined demo. It is very time efficient. You can probably do multiple demos a day, multiple demos a week. And you will never be accused of delaying a deal to develop a custom demo.

Is There Ever a Place for a Canned Demo?

If you sell a relatively straight forward, easy to use solution, a single purpose tool that supports a very specific use case, or a product with minimal options and/or customizations and configurations, then a canned demo probably makes sense. If that's the case, it is reasonable to expect that most prospects will have similar objectives and will be dealing with the same challenges and issues. However, this might also be a good scenario for a recorded demo available on the website. In fact, this is becoming more and more prevalent for standard product demos. If that really is the case, a live demonstration is becoming less desirable – for both buyer and seller.

Overpreparing

Is it even possible to over-prepare? The answer my friends is a resounding yes! It is very possible. In fact, it is one of the most common and most detrimental mistakes I see made. How does this happen, and why is it a problem?

Again, we are engineers by trade. We like to build things. We like to tinker. We like to solve problems. For many in this role, the work they do in preparation of a demo is their favorite part of the job. They can bury themselves deep into a complex solution or example.

The problem is that as a result of our 'deep dive,' the preparation phase of the demo simply takes too long. We are now becoming the bottleneck in the sales process. We run the risk of delaying sales opportunities. This has the potential to affect us personally and financially, because it may limit the number of deals we can work on – which will impact our earnings. We run the risk of over-engineering and over-complicating the demonstration. We also run the risk of developing more than we can show during the time allotted for a demo.

If there's anything I've learned to be true, it's that when we are in front of an audience, we are inclined to demonstrate whatever it is that we've built – regardless of whether there's enough time. As a result, once we get into the demonstration with the customer, we may press to get everything finished. We may end up feeling rushed. We may not allow time for questions so we can show everything we built. This has the potential to be a big problem. Be very wary of this.

Too much content may also force us to be overly precise with our script – just to make sure we can fit everything in, even to the extent that we feel pressed to memorize the script. Which is simply a poor technique. It prevents us from being able to pivot and turn. We end up focusing too much on what we are going to say and not enough on what's happening in the room, or how our customers are responding, etc. For all these reasons, over preparation can be a very bad thing.

Don't Build Content that Won't Be Shown

The other related problem that sales engineers are notorious for is burning countless cycles developing demo content that is NEVER going to be shown. They spend time creating data, views, reports, screens, etc. that will never end up being used in a demo because it's just too much. Therefore, it's important to use what you're actually going to demonstrate as the boundary for what you spend time building. *Don't build more than you can show.*

Is There a Difference Between a Complex Demo and Overpreparing?

Yes. Please don't mistake preparing for complex demonstrations as "over preparation." There are times that a demonstration will require extensive preparation. You may sell a highly complex solution or software platform. You may have an opportunity with a strategic account or customer, or a very large opportunity. Maybe there are numerous stakeholders involved, each with different interests and objectives. It may be a lengthy sales cycle. Or maybe you are working on content that will become part of the post-sales implementation, or the content and script can be reused by other SEs. Certainly, there are times when extensive customized demo content development and preparation is justified. However, we still need to be efficient with our time and effective with our approach.

Focusing on the Wrong Thing – Content Only

The third mistake SEs tend to make when preparing for demos is a hybrid of the first two. Sometimes we focus exclusively or primarily on the demo content development, and we overlook or dismiss preparing the demo script or story. Again, we're engineers. We like to build and tinker. For many in this role, it's much easier to think about the technology than it is to think through the *presentation* of what we've built.

As a result, our demos may sound something like this:

1. Here's what I built.
2. Here's how it looks.
3. Do you get it?
4. Are you impressed?
5. Do you like it?

Ok. So that's an exaggeration, but hopefully you get the point. If we pay too much attention to the content, and not enough attention to the story we are going to tell, chances are our audience isn't going to understand. They aren't going to see how it applies to them. We are leaving too many things to chance. We need a better plan.

Solution

So, what's the solution? What should we be striving for? The most effective SEs strive for balance. They take the time to develop, create, and assemble the demo content required to get the technical win – making sure they are putting their best foot forward. They do what they can to give themselves the opportunity to win. But they are highly efficient with their time. They build no more than they can show in the allotted time – and no more than their audiences can digest in that time. And they balance that with time spent developing the demo script or story. Whether they create custom content or not, they almost always think through the story they are going to tell and spend time laying out a demo script – even if just a loose outline or plan for what they are going to say. They build a story that positions the software in the context of their customers' objectives, requirements, constraints, etc. They create a custom-built story designed specifically for who they are talking to.

How do we achieve this balance?

First, you need to determine whether custom content is required in order to get the technical win or not. This will likely depend on the complexity of the solution you sell. In order to do this, you need to review your notes from the technical discovery call. If you conducted that correctly, you should know the following:

- What custom content is required to be developed and to what extent
- The customers' objectives – this should drive the overall theme and purpose of the demo
- Requirements/priorities – tells you what features/functions/capabilities you need to present
- Constraints – indicates what aspects you can or should omit
- History/Context – indicates competitive positioning you need to consider

Develop a Plan

Armed with these insights and knowledge, you will have what you need to develop a demo plan. The demo plan is your plan for success. Without it, you may burn countless hours trying to get it right. You risk burnout. You risk building too much. You risk focusing on the wrong things. Frankly, you risk making the mistakes we just talked about. Far too many times sales engineers dive into development without *first* taking the time to think through, scope, and outline exactly what it is that they need to build.

Here's what you need to do to build your plan:
- Develop a demo *content* plan
- Develop a demo script *outline*
- *Collaborate/negotiate* with your sales counterpart
- *Commit* to the plan
- *Schedule* the demo

Developing the demo content plan

Before jumping into 'build mode,' go back to the notes from the Technical Discovery Call to determine the following:
1. Custom Data – do you need to build out custom data to drive certain behavior, or to produce required views or reports?
2. Business Context – does the industry example or business scenario matter to your audience or will the standard demo context suffice?
3. Look and Feel Customization – will a customized appearance – logos, color schemes, etc. – be required?
4. Capability Gaps, Shortcomings – were there requirements that will require some level of development to address? Think the "3 C's" - configuration, customization, coding

Once you've asked and answered these four questions, review the list. Now for each item in the list, how long is it going to take to build each one, and in what order do they need to be built? This becomes your plan. Tally up the time, and that is the amount of time you need for the demo content portion of your prep time. Remember, this is just the time to develop the content. You also need to allow time to develop the demo script. (And practice – which is Habit #4. We'll get to that in the next chapter.)

Planning the Demo Script

In this planning stage, we now need to sketch out an outline of the demo story. Do this BEFORE you begin working on demo content. This is an important point. Do not begin working on demo content before you have fully thought through the script. You may discover that it is going to take too long to present what you thought you were going to build. If you can't come up with a concise story and script, you may have to dial back what you were planning to build.

Go back to your list from the prior step. Think through the key things you need to demonstrate. Then write an outline of the flow of the demo, taking into consideration the overall theme and objective. For each item in the outline, assign an estimated time to each key point that you need to make. For example, if there are five key points you want to make in your demo, and each one will take about five minutes, that's a 25-minute demo without any interruptions or questions.

Now ask yourself this question. Will you have enough time to get through the demo in the time allotted and still have time for discussion, interruptions, and questions? If so, great. You have your plan, and you're ready to move on to the next step. If not, revisit your plan for demo content and reevaluate the demo script. Go back and forth between the two until you have balance between them. You don't want to build more than you can demonstrate in the time you have.

Allow Time for Questions

Something to keep in mind: it's critical to allow for questions and discussion during a demo. As a good rule of thumb, the planned demonstration script should require no more than half the amount of time allotted for the demo. For example, if you are being given 30 minutes to demonstrate. Your script should take no more than 15 minutes to complete – if that. This leaves ample time for questions and discussion. It's always better to finish a little early and leave extra room for Q&A than it is to pack too much into your timeslot and not finish the demo or feel rushed.

SEs notoriously try to do too much. We attempt to build more than we can show. We attempt to show more than we have time for. Trust me, I know this from personal experience. Don't be that person. Err on the side of "less is more." If your audience likes what they see, but doesn't get a chance to see everything, they will invite you back for more. If you try to show them too much, and it's overwhelming or feels rushed or forced, you may not be invited back at all.

Collaborate, Commit, and Schedule

Once you have completed the content plan and demo script outline, review them with your sales counterpart. Be sure to explain your strategy and approach, and the overall theme or purpose of your demo. Ensure that it aligns with his or her strategy and approach. Call attention to the specific features, functions, and capabilities you plan to demonstrate, and again be sure that it aligns with what he/she expects to be shown. Allow time to discuss and negotiate any points of disagreement and/or confusion. Keep in mind, that, although we are responsible for the technical win, and it's our job to recommend a technical approach, they ultimately own the opportunity. If you reach an impasse, they have the final say on the approach.

Once you've agreed to the content, approach and storyline of the demo, discuss the time needed to develop everything – the content, material, and script. Keep in mind that he/she will very likely be motivated to have this done as soon as possible. You on the other hand will likely want to pad the schedule a little bit to allow for variance. It's a give and take. Know where your boundaries are. Make recommendations and then negotiate accordingly. Once you've reached an agreement, commit to the date and keep it.

Preparing Demo Content

Here is a list of the best practices in the context of building the content – data, screens, views, behaviors, configurations – for your demo.

- Do as little custom demo content development as possible
- Create custom content ONLY if it's necessary in order to get the technical win
- Be sure the size of the deal outweighs the COST and TIME to develop and deliver
- If it *is* required/justified, be sure to NEGOTIATE enough time
- Develop ONLY that content necessary for the demonstration
- Include ONLY the number of things that can be shown in the given timeframe
- Beware of over-engineering, over-complicating the solution
- The goal is to make it look easy, not complex
- If applicable and available, get and include sample data from the customer

The Rule of the Capital "T"

Another best practice to follow when building out your demo is to follow the rule of the Capital T. This is the principle of "big in appearance, light in content."

In order to understand this concept, let's begin by looking at the opposite. Consider an iceberg. What's on top of the water correlates to what the user sees. It pales in comparison to what's below the surface in the context of software. That's the data, the code, the configurations, the documents, pages, views, etc. The image below reflects this concept visually.

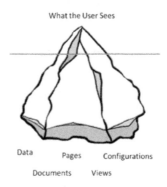

Figure 5: Iceberg, the wrong way to prepare for a demo

When we are building our demos, we do not want to follow this approach. We do not build out the entire "iceberg" under the water in order to show just a few things to the customer, that which is "above the water." (I recognize that for some software solutions this may be a necessity – to do a great deal of work "under the covers" in order to demonstrate the capabilities of the platform. But in most cases, this rule applies.)

Now consider a capital T. The top of the T is what the prospect sees. It's what we are going to show our audience during the demonstration. We go as broad as necessary to meet all their objectives and address all their requirements, but we stay as shallow as possible in terms of what's under the covers. However, where we do need to go deep, that is, if there are sections of the demo in which we need to drill deep into a specific scenario, we can build out that one example but stay reasonably narrow.

Consider this example. Let's say that you sell a case management platform. You might show views that list hundreds or thousands of cases by type or region, etc. You might have graphics and analytics in a dashboard that show key insights and support executive decision making. However, you may also have the need to drill into a specific case in the context of the demo to show specific data points or capabilities within in the tool. In this case you do NOT need to have a complete collection of data below each one of the cases. Just build out a few examples to the "*Nth* degree", and when you need to drill deep, drill deep into those.

As such, demos should follow the rule of the capital "T." Go broad enough to cover all the requirements, but only "ankle deep." Where you do need to drill down, build out just a narrow scope as to limit the amount of time it's going to take. The figure below represents this graphically.

What the Prospect Sees

Data
Pages
Documents
Views
Configurations

Figure 6: Capital T, the right way to prepare for a demo

Preparing the Demo Story

To summarize, here is a list of the best practices in the context of building the script or story:

- The script is the plan for what you are going to say, when, and in what order
- Your demo should tell a story
- It should be based on the outcome your customer is trying to achieve
- It must highlight the solution your product provides
- It must be backed by specific capabilities that make it possible
- It should highlight the features that make your solution unique
- Know your 'ah-ha' moments – there should be 3-5 compelling moments in every demo
- Remember, technical presales is not training (You are not teaching how to use the tool.)
- Show that you understand their objective and give them the solution to get them there

Storytelling Best Practices

Here is a sample outline that lays out a series of storytelling best practices. Use this as a guide when you are building your demo script.

1. **Establish the problem statement**
   a. What is the current harsh reality?
   b. Why is this bad?
   c. Identify the symptoms
   d. Empathize
2. **Give hope**
   a. Describe the "utopian solution"
   b. Give them a vision for the future

   c.   Address symptoms specifically
3. **Demonstrate the vision**
   a.   Lead with the result – what does that utopia look like?
   b.   Show them the "magic behind the curtain"
   c.   Give them the taste of success, happiness, and freedom

Pass the "So What?" Test

The final thought I will leave you with in this chapter on how best to prepare for a complex software demonstration is to pass the "So What?" test. What is the "So What?" test you ask? Review your demo script and consider each point you are going to make. Consider each screen you are going to show. Every behavior or link you are going to call attention to. For each one, ask yourself, *"So what? Why would someone care about that? Why should someone care about that?"* In other words, we are asking ourselves, what is the point we are trying to make here? Why are we showing this?

First, if you can't adequately answer the question for any given step in the demo, you should probably consider removing it. Furthermore, the answer to each question is designed to shift your mindset – from the person who built it or designed it to that of the person who is going to consume it or benefit from it. It is from this perspective that we should be presenting the solution. Rather than saying *"This is what it does"*, for example, we should be saying, *"This is why this is important"* or *"This is why you should care."* It TOTALLY changes the game.

The problem so many of us in this role have, is that we know our solutions so well – sometimes too well. It's easy for us to take certain things for granted. It's easy for us to make too many assumptions. We know the 'special sauce' under the covers. We know the complexity of what went into the system design. We get wrapped up in the bells and whistles. To put it simply, we get wrapped up in ourselves – our product, our solution. All the customer cares about is *"will this solve our problems and/or help us achieve our objectives?"* And if so, is it a better solution than others they've seen? Is it better than the status quo? That's what they are looking for, and that's what we have to demonstrate to get them to say 'Yes' – to get the Technical Win.

Habit #3 Action Plan and Take-aways

Develop the habit of preparing for demos with effectiveness and efficiency. It requires focus and discipline. The key is to remember the difference between preparing WHAT you are going to show (the *demo content*) vs. what you are going to SAY, and how and when you are going to say it (the *demo story*). Prepare extra or custom content *only* as necessary. Focus more on customizing the demo story. Prepare content with the story in mind. Remember, we tend to prepare more material than we can show in the time we have. As a result, we end up rushing through the most important content, and we water down our most important messages. Have the discipline to prepare as necessary but resist the temptation to over-prepare. Focus on your customer and their requirements, not your solution and what you like to talk about or demonstrate.

Action plan to develop this habit:

1. Build demo content plan and demo script outline based on what you heard during technical discovery
2. Strike a balance between the two
3. Negotiate enough time to prepare
4. Do so diligently and efficiently
5. Be sure to leave time to work on the demo story
6. Avoid preparing more than you can show in the time you have
7. Aim to fill 50% of your allotted time with demo content
8. Remember the rule of the Capital T
9. Avoid the iceberg affect
10. Remember, often times, *Less is More*

CHAPTER 5

HABIT #4 - PRACTICE

I'd like you to picture this scene. You're walking into an impressive building in southern California on a warm spring afternoon. It's the corporate headquarters of a well-known Fortune 500 company. The grass out front is perfectly manicured. The leaves of the palm trees in front are swaying gently from a light, warm breeze blowing. You and your sales counterpart are there for a sales presentation and demo. It's the culmination of weeks of planning and preparation. The two of you have worked together for years and have a great partnership. You're a great "one-two punch", as they say. A few weeks back you hosted a technical discovery call and have a very good understanding of what the customer is looking for. More importantly, you're confident you know what you need to show, say, and do to get the technical win. You have your demo built, and your story is ready. Everything is set up for success.

The expected participants are in the room – about 8 people from the prospective company – and the meeting begins. Your colleague opens with a handful of slides. The customer is engaged and attentive. He gets to his final slide and hands the stage to you. You launch into you demo and give a brief intro. You describe your understanding of the issues they are trying to address and empathize with their predicament, explaining that it's something you see regularly. You call attention to a few of the common symptoms of what they are dealing with and ask, "How would it be if you could only do _____?" (I'll let your imagination fill in the blank.)

At this point you have your audience at the ready. They were drawn in by the opening presentation your sales counterpart gave. They are convinced that you understand their challenges, and they're excited to see the solution you are going to unveil. You've built the intrigue, and they're eager to see what you're about to show them – to see what's on the other side of the click.

Click.

Nothing.

Click.

Nothing. Again.

Click. (One more time.)

You wait a little longer. Still nothing.

Sweat starts to bead on your forehead. Your ears turn red. As does your face. "*I don't understand this. It was just working last week.*", you quietly think to yourself. "*What the HELL is going on here?*"

Thinking quickly on your feet you gather yourself and explain what they should have seen. You make some lame excuse about something must not be set up right and move on to some other points. Fortunately, the rest of the demo goes without a hitch, but you know you were rushing through the rest of the demo hoping that the remaining clicks weren't going to leave you hanging like that first one. The meeting closes, they thank you for your time, and thank you for the demo. You apologize for the first part that didn't work, and they say, "Don't worry about it. We can imagine what it was supposed to do." But you know in your heart that there's an element of doubt. So does your colleague. What should have been a walk-off home run was a base hit at best. The audience may have been impressed, but clearly, they're not ready to buy. And no technical win. Not yet.

As you drive out of the parking lot with your colleague you pop open the laptop because you've got to figure out what went wrong. You go to that page that failed in front of the customer and, like a bolt of lightning, it hits you. Two days earlier you reconfigured something and it changed some settings. All you needed to do was point to a new image (or something trivial). It was a 5 second fix. Your system failed in front of the customer at the worst time possible, because of a configuration setting that would have taken you one simple click to find and 5 seconds to fix.

Had you only spot-tested your demo that morning – something you had more than enough time to do, you would have found the issues, fixed it, and delivered a flawless demo. Instead, it bombed in front of the customer and you left them with an element of doubt in their mind.

Does this story sound familiar? Have you ever experienced anything like this? I have. More times than I'd like to remember. And I've seen it happen to others. Enough to know that this isn't an anomaly. It's common place. Does an issue like this during a demo mean the death of the deal? Not necessarily. But it can delay deals. It can introduce doubt and uncertainty. At the very least, it is no fun to be standing in front of a room full of people and have the demo not work as expected.

The ONE Thing We Don't Want After a Click

What's the ONE thing we don't want on the other side of a click? A SURPRISE! Whenever I give a demo, I want to know, without a fraction of a doubt, that when I click into that key page or critical link, that what I'm *expecting* to happen or appear is EXACTLY what is going to happen or appear. We don't want any surprises! And how do we avoid surprises? PRACTICE!

The fourth habit of highly effective sales engineers is to PRACTICE before the demo – to make sure that everything is set up and running correctly.

This may seem obvious to many, if not all of you. You may be thinking of course we should practice before we give a sales demonstration, particularly if it's a complex technology, or it's a large opportunity, or a large audience, with a lot on the line. One might think. But, from my experience in working with and coaching SEs for years, and frankly from my own experience out in the field, practice is often the first thing that drops. When we're pressed for time – and we often are, it's the first thing that's overlooked. We scramble to finish preparing for the demo – pulling all the pieces together, and often go in praying that everything is going to work.

In Chapter 4 we talked about the importance of preparation, and the difference between preparing demo content and the demo script or story. From my experience, almost invariably, when we have a limited amount of time to prepare, and a complex demo to give, we spend as much time as we can on the content and story. We try to maximize our time and include as much as we can in a demonstration, but we tend not to budget time to practice. As a result, we go in with an element of doubt. We go in leaving some things to chance.

So, how do we avoid this? How do we avoid those moments described above, or at least mitigate the risk as much as possible? Before a demo – especially an important demo for a large audience, follow this rule - "Click Every Click."

Click Every Click

Am I suggesting that you literally click every single click that you are going to make in front of your audience? Not necessarily. In many cases that's not realistic and may not be possible. There is virtually no way to predict exactly where your audience might take you with their questions. However, what I'm suggesting here is, at a minimum, click every key click you know you will make.

In the context of your demo script, as we discussed last chapter, there will likely be 3-5 "ah-ha moments". Those key moments in the demo where you are looking for a response, looking to "set the hook". Presumably, each one of those moments will involve some sort of lead in or set up, before the "click" that unveils the magic. It is those steps in the demo – those clicks of the mouse – that we want to be certain are working before we go in to do the demo. For it is those 3-5 points in your demo that explicitly address the customers' needs, set your product apart from the rest, and invariably will make or break the demo.

When I say, "click every click," that's what I'm referring to. It's really a *spot check* of sorts. But a spot check on the most important moments of the demo. And if any one of those key points is a three or four or five step process, click all the way through in advance to make sure everything is working correctly.

Is this really that important?

Glad you asked. Let's ask an even better question. Why do you suppose this is even a problem? Why is it that we find ourselves in these predicaments anyways? From my experience, some part of the system, or network, or configuration has changed since the last time you clicked into that feature. Or someone has changed some data and it no longer produces the result we expect. Or someone has upgraded a component that the system relies on. The bottom line is that someone, somewhere has changed something that affects what you have built unbeknownst to you. Or even worse, you changed something and forgot – it's happened to me dozens of times. Or you've changed something in one place and didn't realize that it would affect something else, somewhere else, and you're just now discovering it – in front of the customer.

I've seen things as simple as running the same exact demonstration but on a new or different laptop make things blow up or not run right. The speed of the internet connection may have an impact on the demo. Using a different web browser can cause problems. Projecting on a new monitor can change the look and feel. The list goes on and on. Again, bottom line, practice the demo – clicking all the most important clicks – using the exact hardware, software, network connection, etc. that you will be using during the demo, if at all possible, of course. Sometimes it may not be.

What if someone steers me down a path I haven't tested?

Good question! Let's discuss that. You're in the middle of a demo and someone in the audience asks a question that steers you down a path in the software that you haven't tested in a while or don't know particularly well? You're now venturing into an unknown territory – an area where there just might be a surprise on the other side of the click. Use your best judgment here. You need to weigh the risk and reward of clicking into a specific screen, page, or function that you're not sure of.

Here's the typical scenario. You're telling your demo story, flowing through your script, clicking through the various key points you planned to demonstrate, and someone asks a question about something that will take you down an unplanned path. (We often refer to this as being led down a rabbit hole, so be cautious of this to begin with). I have a "check down system" that I use before I risk clicking into something that may or may not be working.

The "Check Down" System

First, if someone asks a question that is tangential to the story, respond with a simple answer – a *verbal* answer, not a demonstrable answer. One of the mistakes I see SEs make is they will get totally derailed by a random, "one off" question. They will go down an entirely new path through the software in attempt to answer the question visibly – often wasting countless minutes in the process. Then after what seems like an eternity, the person who asked the question and patiently endured the long-winded response politely says, *"So the answer was yes?"*

Don't make that mistake. When someone asks a question that takes you off the story – and may take you into an untested, unverified portion of the software – respond first with a simple verbal response. That's *check down #1.*

If they, press a little further and say, *"Well, can I see it?"* At that point, we still may not want to have our story or script completely and totally derailed by the question – particularly if we're concerned about whether it's working and/or whether this thread is in the best interest of the customer or the discussion. It may very well be an unnecessary distraction. However, we don't want to come across rude, and we certainly don't want to look like we're trying to avoid something or hide something in the tool. So, at that point, if they press a little more, I would be inclined to show them some evidence of where and how that works – maybe the button or drop-down menu that provides that functionality – but still not go fully into the function. In doing so, I'm now providing some *visible evidence* that the tool does what they are asking for, but I'm not wasting unnecessary time to demonstrate it. More importantly, I'm not putting the demo at risk drilling into something that hasn't been tested or practiced. This is what I refer to as *check down #2.*

If the person asking the question is still not satisfied with the response and wants to see this work, we now have a decision to make. Do we drill in and depart from our planned story and script, or somehow steer it back? Incidentally, in case you are wondering, I've been presented with this scenario dozens of times. Someone asks a question. I respond with a short verbal answer. They ask to see it. I show them a drop-down menu with the option, but don't actually click into it. Still unsatisfied, they press further and say, *"Well can I see how it actually works?"*

As a rule of thumb, if you can make one or two more clicks and show it to them quickly, without steering too far off course, do so – provided you're reasonably confident it's going to work. Conversely, if it's likely to take the conversation way off course – that is, you're headed down the proverbial rabbit hole – or if you're sincerely concerned about whether that feature is working, setup, configured right, etc., find a way to wiggle yourself out of that corner by saying something like the following:

> *"In the interest of time, is it OK for the moment to accept that it works the way I'm suggesting? I've shown you the menu option, so you can see that it is something we've built into the platform. However, it can take a few minutes to set up and click through, and I don't want to detract from the other key points we are here to talk about. Of course, I'd be more than happy to address this in more detail at the end of the meeting, if there's time or after the fact."*

If they really press and/or if the person asking the question is key to the opportunity, then it may very well justify venturing down that rabbit hole. At this point, it would be incumbent upon your sales counterpart to interject and help you navigate through this potentially sticky part of the demo.

To summarize, the *check down system* is a method for how to respond when someone in your audience asks a question about the software that you had not planned to show. Remember the 3-Vs – Verbal, Visual, Vivid Detail.

1.   First, provide a *VERBAL* answer

2. Second, show *VISUAL* evidence briefly (drop-down menu, button, etc.)
3. Third, go into *VIVID DETAIL* (only if they press, and only if you determine benefit outweighs the risk)

Confidence

The key point on Habit #4 is this: you want to be entering each demo with a high level of *confidence* that the key moments in your demo – the most important clicks of the mouse you are going to make – are going to work correctly. You do this by doing a quick practice run the night before or the morning of, spot checking those key clicks to make sure everything is running as expected. If someone asks a question that takes you into an area of the software that hasn't been spot tested, use a "check down" approach to answer the question quickly, and avoid the risk of clicking into a surprise.

INSIGHT: I'm of the belief that the way in which we respond to questions – how we react, what we say, and how we say it – may very well be the most important thing we do in a demonstration. From my experience, it is the one skill that determines the outcome of a sales demonstration, more than any other. In the next chapter, we will cover this extensively. For now, suffice it to say that it's important to be alert and avoid being unnecessarily led down a "rabbit hole" when someone asks a question about something that's beyond what you planned to demonstrate.

Should I expect perfection?

No. Of course not. We will we run into problems from time to time. A transaction will die. A page won't be found. A process will hang. Some data will be missing. Etc. Etc. Software is not perfect. It tends to be finicky, especially in front of prospects and customers. So, no, having confidence does not mean expecting perfection. However, if you've prepared properly, like we discussed in the last chapter, and have practiced, as we're discussing here, those moments should be few and far between, and hopefully not during one of the more important moments of the demo. But issues will surface. So, don't beat yourself up when you have a few bumps in the road.

What do I do when something does go wrong?

Good question. Let's first consider what we should not do. Here is a list of things to not to do when something goes wrong.

1. Don't panic. It is what it is. Something has gone wrong. Getting emotionally worked up and flustered is only going to make things worse.
2. Don't blame the tool. Do not make it appear as though there is anything wrong with the software.
3. Don't say, *"Ugh! Again? I don't understand why this keeps happening!"* That would be very bad. (We don't want this to look like a common thing.)
4. Don't act like nothing has happened or that nothing is wrong – unless of course it isn't obvious to the audience. If it's obvious to everyone in the room that something isn't working, but you act like there's no problem, they will see through that, and you will lose credibility.
5. Don't freeze like a deer in headlights. Everyone in the room is looking to you to carry the group through this awkward, disappointing moment.
6. Don't crawl into a mental bubble, stare at your computer, and block the rest of the world out.
7. Don't think aloud or start murmuring to yourself.
8. Don't spend too much time trying to solve the problem.
9. Don't attempt to reconfigure, code, compile, etc. the demo in front of your audience. (One of the worst things we can do is show the "underbelly" of the software to new prospective client, i.e., the admin page, custom scripting language, XML, etc.)
10. Don't over explain or attempt to justify what happened, lest "thou doth protest too much."

11. Don't make issues bigger than they are. If you can't get something to work, move on.
12. Don't allow issues to ruin the rest of the demo.

Wow! That's a long list!

Yes. And there are probably a few other things we could add to the list if we gave it some more thought. There are numerous ways not to handle a situation when something doesn't work. Hopefully, you get the point. It's bad enough when the software doesn't do what we expect it to do. How we react or respond will ultimately dictate how big or small of a deal it really is.

OK, so what should I do?

Below is a list of things you *can* do to navigate your way through the most awkward of moments with grace and finesse.

1. Stay calm. Something didn't work as expected. The best-case scenario is that you can diagnose and fix it in a matter of seconds, and then continue with the demo. You give yourself a much better chance of doing that by staying calm.
2. Act surprised and/or confused. You want to give the impression that this issue is unusual and atypical. (Whether it is or not.)
3. Look at the audience, apologize, and acknowledge the problem.
4. Blame yourself. "I must have done something wrong here." This takes the impetus off the software.
5. Very quickly attempt to diagnose and fix the problem. ONLY if you can do so without exposing an ugly administrative view of the tool. If you can fix it, great. Do so and continue.
6. Know when to "punt". Know when to skip and move on.
7. If you can fix it, explain briefly what happened, so the audience understands.
8. If you cannot fix it, tell your audience what you think the problem is, and explain that it would only take about 5 minutes to fix but you don't want to bore them with that.

9. Use what happened to your advantage, if possible. As an example, something didn't work because you didn't have the correct security permissions. Take that opportunity to show that that was an example of the security controls in action.
10. Have a canned response at the ready whenever you have an issue with a demo – so you're not caught off guard.

That's a lot to remember. Can you give an example of this in action?

Absolutely. Assume for a moment that you sell business intelligence software. You are about to show a compelling chart designed to display a range of information pertaining to how certain products are performing in certain geographical areas, along a wide range of demographic information. It's a killer visual graphic – one of your ah-ha moments. You set it up effectively, talking about the challenges your customer is trying to address. The business insights they are trying to gain and explain that with one magical click of the button, they are going to have a view of their business that they've never had before. Click. Nothing. Your response might sound something like this:

> *"Wow. I didn't see that coming. This is very unusual. That was sort of anti-climactic, wasn't it? I must have done something wrong. Ah, my apology. I wasn't logged in under the correct ID and didn't have the right permissions. Let me log out and log back in under the right ID. In the meantime, allow me to call attention to our security model. As you just saw in real time, you can limit who has access to specific reports and information in the platform."*

Let's break that down. What were the rules in play there?
1. The response was calm.
2. It showed a sense of surprise but acknowledged the issue.
3. It was self-effacing and put the blame on self not the tool.
4. There was a brief apology.

5. There was a brief explanation.
6. Then it was turned into an opportunity to introduce the security measures built into the platform – which is a good thing, not a bad thing.

In this example, a potentially horrific moment in the context of the demo became a small bump in the road. In fact, it was spun into a positive moment, by drawing attention to the security model, and became part of the flow. We know, however, that it isn't always that easy. Sometimes it won't be a quick fix like that. Sometimes you won't be able to shift on the fly and keep going. What then?

We're still going to follow the guidelines above. Remain calm. Assess the issue as quickly as possible, and if you're at an impasse, move on. This is also a moment in which the relationship you have with your sales counterpart is critically important. If you and your sales rep are working as partners, you will have dealt with issues like this before, and will have discussed and agreed upon how you should handle these situations. Does he or she prefer that you forge ahead? Does he or she want to get involved in the discussion? Remember, at the end of the day, they own the account. They own the opportunity. From my experience, all sales reps have their own way of dealing with technology issues during a demo. Part of being a good partner is discussing that before you're in front of a customer.

No software application or platform is perfect. All software packages have their flaws and limitations. Sales reps often have a harder time accepting this than we do. They never want to see the software they are selling come up short. They always want to be able to say yes to a customer. But that's simply not realistic. Please do not put pressure on yourself to be perfect in every demo or to expect perfection from the software you sell. It's OK if the software doesn't address every one of a customers' questions or needs. It's OK if the demo doesn't come off perfectly. What matters far more is how you respond to and handle those issues in the moment. (And yes, whatever those moments are, and how closely related to a customers' objectives and requirements they are, matters too).

That being said, *WE* don't want to be the reason something bombed in front of a customer. If the reason something went wrong is because we just didn't do our due diligence in advance, then that's on us. And THAT's what we need to make every effort to eliminate and avoid.

Habit #4 Action Plan and Take-aways

In summary, practice your demos. Click every click – the important ones. Spot check. Leave NOTHING to chance. The one thing we don't want after a click is a SURPRISE. Be sure what you are practicing on is precisely what will be demonstrated for the customer. Practice on the laptop you will be using, with the projector or resolution you will be presenting, on the right version of the software, against the same server, using the same data, etc. Treat it like a dress rehearsal. Nothing should be different than what you will be working on in front of the customer.

If something does go wrong, know how to respond. Turn large bumps in the road into insignificant pebbles. Give yourself every opportunity to get the Technical Win.

Action plan to develop this habit:
1. Budget time to practice
2. Do a dry run with your sales counterpart
3. Click every click
4. Don't fuss with your demo and make last minute changes
5. Test the same configuration you will use with the customer
6. Spot test the morning of the demo

CHAPTER 6

HABIT #5 – PERFORM (PART 1)

Let's review what we have covered so far in this book. We opened with the notion that we are in sales and talked about the importance of having that mindset. We established the goal of technical presales which is to get the *Technical Win*. We have talked through the first four habits, which are:

- Habit #1 – to PARTNER with our sales counterparts and develop an effective working relationship. The central theme being "Sales is a team sport".
- Habit #2 – to PROBE into customer requests for a demonstration to understand their objectives, requirements, etc. and the importance of hosting a Technical Discovery Call.
- Habit #3 – to PREPARE with both effectiveness and efficiency in mind, by understanding the critical difference between demo content vs. the demo script.
- Habit #4 – to PRACTICE before any given demo – especially for large, strategic opportunities, and the technique of "click every click".

If we were to classify these four habits and the techniques and best practices related to them, they would fall under the heading of "pre-demo activities" or "pre-demo best practices". They are all related to what happens before the demo. They are critically important to and will go a long way towards ensuring our success. But at the end of the day, at some point, the spotlight is going to be on us. Our sales counterpart is going to say what he or she has to say, for better or for worse, and then they are going to 'hand the mic' over to us. And when that happens, we need to be ready to PERFORM.

I'm not necessarily saying we need to put on an act, (although certainly some showmanship is involved). In fact, I'll go a step further and suggest quite the contrary. Acting is pretending to be someone you are not. I'm not suggesting that at all. I encourage all the SEs I work with to BE YOURSELF. The worst thing you can do is try to be someone else or be someone you're not. If you're loud and gregarious, be loud and gregarious. If you're naturally low key or have a dry sense of humor, be that in front of your audience.

The most effective SEs recognize a demonstration as a performance. We are on stage, and it's our job to get our prospects excited about our solution. It's our job to enable them to see how our solution will help them solve their problems or meet their objectives. It's our job to get them to say YES. What I have learned (and seen) over the years is that there are very specific techniques that we can apply – that we NEED to apply – to dramatically increase our results.

More importantly, these are practices that will make your job more enjoyable and more fulfilling, not to mention, enable you to sell more software and make more money. It will also make the experience that much more satisfying for your prospects and customers. In addition, you will be enabling them to make better purchase decisions – which of course, we hope is in our favor. It has been proven time and time again that the best product doesn't always win. But more times than not, the best demo does. How you perform on stage, more times than not, will be the difference between victory and defeat.

If I may, this section arguably could have been a book of its own. In fact, many of the books in print about software demonstrations focus largely on this segment – what to say and how to say it, when presenting to a customer. We will cover a total of 20 tips, techniques and best practices. They are organized into three sections: the pre-demo setup, the delivery, and getting the technical win. The first two are covered in this chapter. The third is covered in the next chapter.

These two chapters will take you from good to great. It is the skills covered in this habit that make you the most highly sought-after SE on the team, because they are the skills that lead to close. They will also draw the admiration and appreciation of your customers. Last but certainly not least, they will give you the confidence to go into any situation and give a stunning software demonstration.

How are you so sure about these techniques?

Good question! You *should* be asking that. My answer is simple. In most cases, I have learned the hard way – by doing the opposite – before I figured it out and learned to do things the right way. (As I say, I've been doing this a long time.) I'm pretty sure I've made every mistake you can possibly make in front of a customer. Or I've seen a colleague make the mistake, or a company pitching me a product make the mistake.

I've also seen and experienced the successes. I've seen a room full of complete and total skeptics do a full 180 and leave the room thanking me for my time. I've won deals that I was told were unwinnable. I've presented to large audiences and small. I've given LONG demonstrations and brief ones. I've presented to adoring fans of our solution and downright hostiles. To be clear, I haven't won every deal I've been a part of. But I've learned what it takes to put the best foot forward – every time. And that's what we should be striving to do.

In sports, they have the saying "leave it all out of the field". That's the way you should be thinking in technical presales. With every demo, you want to "leave it all out on the field". You want to walk away knowing you gave it all you could. Put your best foot forward – that of your company and that of your product – to the best of your ability. There's nothing more you can ask of yourself. By learning, adopting and applying the techniques you are about to see in the pages ahead, that's precisely what you will be able to do.

Are you intrigued? Excited? I hope you are! Let's get started.

Pre-Demo Setup

In this first of three segments of Habit #5 – PERFORM, we will cover the techniques necessary to effectively "tee up" the demo. We have spent a lot of time thus far talking about best practices that we need follow in the days and weeks leading up to a big demo. In this section we are going to discuss some specific techniques we need to apply in the moments leading up to that first click.

Get Agreement Up Front

The first technique is what I refer to as *getting agreement up front*. You can also think of this as setting expectations or establishing context. In fact, you can almost think of this as establishing *boundaries* for what's "in scope" and "out of scope" for the demonstration you're about to give and the ensuing conversation. Allow me to elaborate.

Before you begin a demonstration, you want to get agreement on the objectives they're trying to address, the requirements they're trying to satisfy, the issues they're trying to solve, etc. Even if your sales counterpart has already done so in the context of his or her sales presentation, I suggest that you reiterate what's already been said, but in a subtle and clarifying manor. You might say something like, *"So, as my colleague Matt has stated, the purpose of this brief demonstration is to show you how you can use our solution to accomplish XYZ. We will pay close attention to how we specifically address XYZ issues. At the end of the day I will show you how you can achieve XYZ."*

The next step here is critical. You want to ask for agreement or consent. *"Does that align with your expectations?"* or, *"Will that satisfy what you were hoping to see during today's demonstration?"* What you're doing here is setting a boundary for what's in scope for the session and what's not.

Why is this so important?

It's important for two reasons. Number one, it's almost like drawing up an unwritten, informal contract with the audience over what's fair game for today's demonstration and discussion. This is important, because later in the demonstration if they try to throw you any curve balls, you can use this to your advantage. Number two, if there IS something else, they were expecting to see, or if there is some other objective or requirement, you want to know that up front – BEFORE you get into your demonstration. We all know how hard it is to pivot and shift mid-demo. (And if you don't, you'll find out sooner or later.) So, we want to know – before we get into our flow – is there, in fact, anything else that they have on their agenda, that we were not planning to address?

What do I do if the answer is yes?

If in fact something does come out that has not previously been discussed – and it does from time to time, we now have a decision to make. Is this something we can easily add into the discussion? Is it something you can easily and readily address? If so, then thank them for mentioning it and assure them that you will be happy to include it as part of the demonstration and conversation.

What if it's something that you might be able to include in the demonstration, but could use some additional exploration or clarification? If that's the case, drop into a little bit of discovery – right then and there. My response might go something like this…

"Oh, I don't think we've discussed that up until now." Or *"I don't think that's been mentioned before now. I'm sorry we missed that requirement. Can you help me understand a little bit more about that requirement? Why is that important? What were you hoping to see? In the list of priorities, where does that fall in relation to the other things that we've been talking about?"*

Any one or more of these questions will help tease out how important this new requirement or expectation is. This is SO important. Because it tells us how seriously we need to take this new insight. Their response might be something like *"To be honest, it's no big deal. It was just a passing thought, but it's minor. If we can see it, great. But if not, it's not as important as the other items we've been talking about."*

Or they might say *"Well actually, this is one of the more important aspects of what we're looking for."* Now we know that we might have to completely shift or rearrange the demo and make this the focus. If we can do so on the fly – good news. Let's get started. But what if we can't, well, now we're in a bit of a pickle.

What if they want to see something I can't easily show?

Great question. If it turns out that our audience has an expectation for something that we are unprepared to demonstrate – something comes out moments before we begin our demo, and it's NOT something we can just whip out of our bag of tricks. Well, now we have a bit of a dilemma on our hands. We don't ever want our software to look difficult, and we don't want to miss an opportunity to show a prospect something they are legitimately interested in. But if it's something you just can't pull out on the fly, or something that might not be working properly, you really can't fake it.

My first thought is that this goes back to habit #1, to PARTNER. This is a very good example of a scenario or situation that you should discuss with your sales counterparts in general. Discuss with him or her how they prefer to handle situations like these. Second, when faced with a situation like this, I personally am inclined to be very honest and simply say it's not something I'm prepared to do. I will then look to my sales counterpart for guidance on what to do at this juncture.

The question at hand now is do we move forward with the demonstration as scheduled anyways and show them what we were planning to show them? Or if this is really the most important thing – and really the only or primary thing they are interested in seeing – does it make more sense to reschedule the demo and spend the rest of the time talking more about this important capability that we somehow missed and precisely what it is that they are looking for.

To that end, my response might sound something like this. *"I'm very sorry. I'm simply not prepared to demonstrate that part of the solution or address the specific need or scenario today."* Then, turning to my sales counterpart, I would say, *"What do you suggest we do Bill? Shall we proceed with what we have prepared, or should we consider rescheduling?"*

Wait a minute. If we've done discovery, how is this even possible?

Very astute question. For those of you who have been in this business for a while, you may have experienced something like this. But for those of you who may be newer to this role, you may very well be asking yourself this question. How *is* it possible that we could find ourselves in this situation, assuming we've done qualification and discovery? That at the eleventh hour we would discover an important requirement or objective that went previously unmentioned? I agree that it may be hard to believe. And it should be more the exception than the rule – especially if we are following the steps discussed earlier in the book. But I can assure you it happens.

Typically, it's the result of "new players" entering the meeting – particularly senior members of the team whom we didn't expect. They will come in with *their* agenda, *their* requirements. Sometimes, it just turns out that the folks we've been speaking to and dealing with simply didn't represent the boss – or the boss's boss – and what their objectives are, adequately.

Sounds like you're speaking from personal experience.

Yes indeed. Allow me to give you an example. I was in York, Pennsylvania for a software demonstration. It was about a three-hour drive for me – one way. I was flanked by two sales colleagues – one who was responsible for the account as a whole – so the account executive, if you will, and one who was an overlay sales rep responsible for one of the other product lines. This company was a current customer of the other product line, so the overlay rep was there primarily to make a 'courtesy call' appearance – a 'well baby visit', as I like to say. I was invited by the account exec to give a technical presentation and demo for their Enterprise Architecture team. The product I was representing was newly acquired and the AE was trying to cross sell this new customer. They both gave brief presentations and then handed the floor to me. I had done some technical discovery with the technical principals who I knew would be in the room and felt reasonably confident.

About 20 minutes into my portion of the meeting, the CIO – whom I didn't know was going to be there, and who didn't say much up until that point, turns to me and says, *"Can I see your ability to generate a Technology Roadmap?"* Silence. For what seemed like an eternity. I wasn't prepared to show or even talk about Technology Roadmaps. It was not a strength of the product I was selling at the time. It could be configured to do so, to some degree. But it was certainly not something I could turn on a dime and show.

He caught me completely off guard and frankly, it was obvious. I started back-peddling. I'm sure I started sweating. My face probably turned multiple shades of red. And the meeting went downhill from there. I'm pretty sure we didn't manage to cross-sell that particular customer.

What's the point of the story? Had I done a better job of establishing up front what it was that I was going to be presenting. And verifying that I wasn't missing anything, we would have – at least we should have been able to – tease that requirement out up front, BEFORE I got into my demo flow. I could have drilled into what his requirements were, how important it was, how he expected to use it, etc. etc. I could have explained to him that I wasn't necessarily prepared to show it to him in demonstration, but that with his permission, I would be happy to offer a whiteboard illustration as to how our product generates Technology Roadmaps and offer to send him some examples after the fact. I truly believe it would have been a totally different outcome. But because I didn't tease it out up front – nor did the account exec I might add – I was caught off guard, struggled to come up with the right response and lost control of the meeting.

What if I don't get a response?

If you ask for this clarification up front and don't get a response, do not move ahead until you do. Do not start the demo until you have acknowledgment from the group – or at least your sponsor that yes, that is what they are looking for and expecting to see.

Allow me to restate that for emphasize. *Do not move forward* until you get some sort of response. Your audience may at first, be a little reluctant to respond. And this may happen for a variety of reasons. Remember, you don't know the dynamics in the room on their side. They may have some people in the room that honestly don't have any idea why they've been invited to the meeting. You might have some people in the room that have differing opinions on what the priorities are or what they should be doing. You might have a group that doesn't even know what the purpose is, or expectations are. Or they may be unsure who should answer.

Whatever the case, don't press on until you get a response. I've seen SEs attempt to do the right thing by asking the clarification question up front. Then, launch into their demo without getting a response! That's almost worse than not asking the question to begin with. If you ask and they can't or don't give you a good answer, there's something going on. Figure it out before you launch.

I've literally heard, *"I'll take silence as a yes"* and then watched them forge ahead. NO! Do not take silence as a yes. Silence is not a yes. Do not move forward until someone in the room has acknowledged that yes, that's what we're here to see and that aligns with our expectations. If they can't give you that then maybe you shouldn't be there to begin with.

OK. So how do we do this?

Before you launch into your demo, put up a single slide that says, "This is What We Heard" and list out all the key points that you took away from the *technical discovery call*. Explain that these were the items that you captured during the call, and that it is based on these notes that you have created the demo. Explain that the demo they are about to see is in response to these requirements. We want to verify that we got it right. We want to know if anything has changed since the call. We also want to know if there's anything not on the list that should be. If it's a particularly long list, ask if there are any items that "jump off the page" as most being the most important or most critical to their success.

The final word...

We've done our technical discovery call. We've qualified and prepared accordingly. Now, before we start the demo, we want to make sure, that everyone in the room is on the same page.

There may be some people in the room that were not on the technical discovery call or were not part of the qualification process. We want those individuals to know that we've done our homework. We've already talked to some folks in the group, and this is what we've agreed to present and discuss. It sets boundaries on the scope, which as we will see later in this chapter is very important.

There may be a new player who is a senior member of the team. If that's the case, they may have an agenda that is bigger and broader than what has been discussed to date. If so, we most certainly want to tease that out before we launch into our prepared demo. Do this up front before you begin.

Know the Players

The next best practice in delivering a winning demonstration is to *know the players*. What do we mean by this? Depending of course on the solution you sell, the size of the companies you sell to and other potential dynamics, whenever you give a software demonstration, chances are good that you'll be demonstrating to a group of people, as opposed to just one. Although certainly that happens as well. For arguments sake, let's assume that most of your demos are given to groups of five or more people.

In most cases, you're going to have different people with different perspectives, different roles, different interests, and more importantly different responsibilities in the decision-making process – the *purchase* process. This is particularly true if you sell enterprise software. In fact, studies have shown that in the past five years enterprise software purchase decisions involve more people than ever before.

Why is this important?

Different people with different roles will have different interests and concerns about your software. The way you communicate and respond to one group needs to be very different from how you respond to others. Let's consider some examples.

Some folks in the room will be prospective users of the tool or the platform. They are going to be interested in the specifics and nuances of the tool – how it works, how it will affect their day job, etc. They are going to be more detail-oriented in nature.

You will likely have technical influencers in the room. These are typically technical principals who have significant influence over the technical purchase decision – i.e., the technical win. They will likely be experts in the field and will likely have some very specific questions that they want to have answered. They may be very dogmatic on certain topics like approach, methodology, architecture, etc. Your success will depend on winning over these technical experts.

You will also likely have some key decision makers in the room or on the demo. These may be a project sponsor or executive manager, director, VP, etc. They may or may not ultimately own the budget. In either case, they are typically less interested in the details of the technology. They are looking to determine if an investment in this software is going to produce the desired outcomes. They will look to verify the technical principles are satisfied.

The final category of people in the room to be aware of is a group I refer to as "uninvited guests". These are individuals who are not even part of the decision-making team. They are "people from down the hall" who were invited at the last minute to "hear what the demo guys have to say". Be very wary of this group. They have the potential be disrupt a meeting in a very destructive way, if you are not careful.

Know where the "center of the room" is

We will discuss how to address questions from each one of these groups later in the chapter, but for now, suffice it to say that it is critically important to know who's who in the room and make a mental note accordingly. Know where the *center of the room* is – the most important, most influential, highest ranking member of the team. He or she often holds the key to the budget. At one of my former companies, we called this person "the bully with the juice".

Know also who the *technical influencers* are. Make sure they understand the key capabilities of the software and make every attempt to ensure their questions are addressed to their satisfaction. Know who the potential *users* are – those individuals who will use the software. Their questions will be more specific, detail oriented. Finally, know who the *uninvited guests* are and handle them with caution. Know who falls into which of the four categories listed above and prioritize accordingly.

1. Decision makers
2. Technical influencers
3. Users
4. Uninvited guests

This begins during Technical Discovery

By the way, when does this process begin, the process of understanding who's who? In the technical discovery call of course! We talked about this briefly in that chapter. This is something that should have surfaced during that call. Just as we should be walking into the demo knowing what the requirements are, and what it is that we need to say, show and do. We should be walking in with a pretty good idea of who's who. As such, you should be able to identify new players quickly. Be aware of that and use it to your advantage.

Where does your point of contact stack?

Let's take that a half a step further. Once you get into the room and meet all the players, pay close attention to where the individual you spoke to during the technical discovery call falls in the pecking order. That is an early indicator of how credible and reliable the information he/she provided is, and how well that information represents the voice of the group. The higher that person ranks, the better positioned you are. If it turns out that he/she is lower on the totem pole, it may be that much more important to do some discovery up front and establish those boundaries, establish that agreement on the scope of the meeting.

Begin with introductions

As a best practice, be sure to open the meeting with a round of introductions. This is especially important if you're unsure of who's who. It requires coordination with your sales counterpart. He/she will typically kick off the meeting. Have them open by asking the audience to introduce themselves – their name, their role, and a brief comment on what their expectations for the meeting might be.

It may not be practical to do this every time. If you have a larger room with 20 or more people, you may not have time to do something like that. If that is the case, I would at the very least invite the person who helped you coordinate the meeting make some brief introductions.

Take notes

While the attendees are introducing themselves be sure to have a notepad ready and jot down the name of each individual, along with a note or two about their role, their expectations, etc. Then, throughout your demo you will have this information to refer to. It's incredibly powerful. When someone asks a question, you can glance down at your notes and respond to him/her by using their first name. You also know the context from which the question is being asked, because you know their role and you jotted down what they were hoping to see that day.

Allow me to give you an example. You receive a question from the group. Your response may sound something like, *"Good question, Bob. I recall you said that you were responsible for the infrastructure, so I can see where that question might be coming from. Let me see if I can explain."*

Address people by name and make it personal

I cannot possibly overstate how powerful this is in the context of a demonstration. From my experience, people are incredibly impressed when you pay attention to their name, their roles and their interests. It builds rapport and trust. They are going to begin rooting for you and rooting for your product.

Let's take this a step further. You need *not* wait until one of them asks a question to use this information. During your demo, if there's a key point or feature you plan to call attention to, and you know it aligns with something one of the attendees specifically showed an interest in, you can call on that person by name, proactively. Let's look at another example. We'll stick with our friend Bob. *"As I move on to this next point, allow me to draw your attention to this Bob. You mentioned in the beginning that you're responsible for infrastructure. As such, I think this may be particularly interesting to you."*

Keep them on their toes

Again, what are we doing here? We are showing that we paid attention to them and who they are. We are presenting it in the context of who they are and what they care about. We are also keeping the audience on their toes. Once they realize that you have paid attention to everyone's name and may call upon them at some point, they are going to pay that much more attention. They are going to stay that much more engaged. And frankly, if someone starts to daydream or drift off – which if you're giving a compelling demo, shouldn't happen – calling on them by name draws them right back into the conversation. It's powerful.

This technique cannot be emphasized enough. Know the players. Know their roles. Know where the center of the room is. Address them by name and present your demonstration in the context of what matters most to each of them, to the extent you can.

Be Set Up and Ready to Go

The next best practice to adopt is relatively straight forward, but one that is still worth sharing because of how frequently it seems to be overlooked. This is simply the practice of being ready when called upon. That's it. Simply put, *be set up and ready to go* when the spotlight shines upon you.

In many cases, you will be invited to begin your demo after your sales counterpart has presented a handful of slides – introducing the company, the solution, a case study, etc. When he/she completes their part of the presentation, they will hand the floor to you to begin your demonstration. When this happens, you need to be at the ready to launch straight into your demo.

This probably seems so obvious. But I've seen countless demos in which the SE wasn't ready. Either they had to log into the system. Or they had to "fire up some services". Or they had to navigate through five pages or screens to get to their starting point.

I've even witnessed a demonstration given over the web, in which the sales rep finished his slide presentation a few minutes sooner than expected and switched control of the screen over to the SE that was supporting him. When her screen appeared, it was a flyer that she was working on for a bake sale at her kids' school! She was only paying half attention to the conversation going on – at best. How embarrassing is that?

If you are presenting on the customer's site, in a conference room together, you may very likely be using the same laptop for both the slides presented by the sales rep and the demo you will present. If that is the case, get everything up and running before your sales counterpart launches the slides and begins his/her talk. I realize that something may "time out" in the time that the sales rep is speaking. So, you may have log back in. But other than that, everything should be ready to go.

If it's not possible to have everything up and running in the background for the 10-15 minutes your sales colleague is going to speak, then use two separate laptops. Just be sure that when your colleague is finished that you are logged in and ready to go and make the switch between the laptops as quickly and cleanly as possible.

This is another good example of the importance of the partnership you have with your sales counterpart. Every sales rep I've worked with has had their own style. Some like their own laptop. Some like to share. Some get anxious about switching machines. Etc. Etc. Discuss the logistics up front and make sure the two of you are on the same page.

What's the opposite?

What's the opposite? What is it that we want to avoid? We want to avoid long delays, because we don't want our audience to get bored or distracted during the switch. And we want to avoid looking clumsy. We want to look professional and polished. We want to look like the kind of people they'd like to do business with.

Keep your head in the game

One final comment on this section, while your sales counterpart is giving his/her part of the presentation, keep your head in the game. If you are in the room, pay very close attention to the audience. How do they seem to be responding to the material being presented? Are they engaged? Are they asking questions? If they do, pay close attention to their questions and the answers being offered. This is additional context you can use during your demonstration.

If you are presenting over the web, it's very easy to get distracted while your colleague is speaking – email, fussing with the demo, the flyer for your kid's school. Resist the temptation to do other things while your colleague is speaking – even if you've heard the pitch a hundred times. You've never heard what this audience might have to say, and you can use that to make your demo better. Shut down email, IM and other distractions and keep your focus. Take notes that you can refer to during your segment. Be ready to go when the spotlight shines on you.

The Delivery

Now that we have discussed what it takes to *tee up* the demo effectively, it's time to launch. In this second segment of Habit #5 – PERFORM, we will cover the techniques necessary to effectively *deliver* the demo. You're now on stage, with mouse in hand, under the spotlight. These are the techniques that will make your demo a compelling and memorable performance.

Begin with the End

You have set and verified expectations. You know all the players and you are set and ready to go. The next critical ingredient of a winning demonstration is to *begin with the end*. In fact, this is the key tenet of Peter E. Cohan's method and book, *"Great Demo!"*. As Peter puts it, "do the last thing first". This is something I was first introduced to in the classroom when I went through an internal training program that was based on his book, but something that has been proven to me repeatedly. This approach works. Period!

Why do Peter and I and others like us make such a big deal of this concept? (Brian Geery, another author and recognized expert in the space refers to it as *"making the James Bond entry"*.) Because as SEs, we are SO tempted to tell our audience about all the work it took us to arrive at the results we got. We love to demonstrate how smart we are, and how clever and sophisticated the tool is. But here's the problem. Nobody cares. At least not yet. Not now. All they care about at the outset of the demo is will the software do what we need it to do? And is this guy going to show us something impressive or bore us to death like most of the people we've seen?

When you launch into your demo you want to show the most impressive, most compelling capability, screen, or aspect of your solution – basically the pinnacle – right out of the gate, in the first 2-5 minutes.

The opposite of this is to save it for the end. As if you are building up to some crescendo finish. That may work in movies but not in software demonstrations.

Why is this so important?

Because otherwise your audience will get impatient and bored. Or worse, you may confuse them along the way. They simply aren't interested in all the things that it took to get to a result. They just want to see that it works. When you show them something right out of the gate you get their attention. They're intrigued. Now they want to know how you did what they just saw. It's a totally different experience.

A demo is like a magic trick, with one important distinction

Allow me to share with you one of my favorite analogies. Giving a demo is lot like doing a magic trick, only there's one significant difference.

Something I do in every one of my seminars is a magic trick. And I do it early in my talk. Why? I'm following my own advice – to begin with the end, of course. I explain to the audience that I would like to do a demonstration for them – but not a software demonstration, a different kind of demonstration.

I begin by asking the audience to raise their hands if they have kids. Often, it's most of the room. *"How many of you would like to go home and impress your kids tonight with a magic trick?"*, I ask. Again, most of the hands go up. At this point, I have their attention.

I now launch into my "demo", i.e. magic trick, which usually lasts about a minute or two. I have a couple of go-to tricks, that are quite good, even if I do say so myself. Sometimes I integrate the trick into a story. Sometimes I'll even get some crowd participation. So far, without exception, I've managed to pull off every trick I've done in front of a live audience – without a hitch. And, as best as I can tell, they've all been reasonably impressed with the trick. More importantly, I've sensed that they sincerely had NO IDEA how I actually pulled it off. (That's important.)

I then ask a very poignant next question. *"How many of you would like to know how I did that trick?"* Now, EVERY hand in the room is up. I then go about explaining "the trick" – what it was that I did to pull it off. Invariably, once I've explained how I the trick works, which in every case is incredibly easy and straight forward, I sense two things. One, everyone in the room seems to think, *"Oh? That's it? I can do that."* Two, and this is a key point, they seem to be a little less impressed by my trick. The mystique is gone. Yet, I still sense an eagerness to go home and show their kids!

With that I ask my audience the key question, which at this point seems obvious to me. *"How much LESS impressed would you have been, had I told you what the trick was BEFORE I did the trick?"*

Honestly, almost without exception, you can hear a pin drop in the room after I ask that question. It hits everyone like a ton of bricks. The answer is it would have made all the difference in the world.

If I had told them what the trick was before I did it, they probably wouldn't even have wanted to see it. It's in that moment that many of them realize that what they've been doing all along – how they've been giving demos – is backwards. They show all the things that lead up to the "magic" first, but by then the magic is simply gone.

The *only* difference between a software demonstration and a magic trick, is that we always reveal the secret to the trick after the fact. Magicians do not.

Smoke and Mirrors

I've heard fellow SEs accuse some colleagues as using "smoke and mirrors" to give the illusion of something working a specific way. I say let the smoke and mirrors reign. So long as you show all the smoke and reveal all the mirrors that it took to produce the outcome you produced – after the fact.

Anchor your story to a higher purpose

Another key takeaway from that story is the fact that I opened by asking the audience for a show of hands from those who had kids. Then asked them if they'd like to impress their kids that night with a magic trick.

What did I do there? I upped the ante. I anchored my story to a higher purpose. I related what I wanted to show them with something I knew would be important to them. It wasn't about watching me give a "demo". It was about them learning a trick they could show their kids that night. It totally changes the game when you can connect what you are showing to one of *their* priorities.

Consider the reverse

To emphasize the point, let's consider the reverse. What's the mistake SEs make? They painstakingly walk their audience through 30 or 40 minutes of set up, explanation, configuration, etc. They show all the steps that they took to get to the end point. They finally get to that climactic point 30 or 40 minutes into the demo.

Chances are they've lost the audience along the way. Or they have confused their audience. Or the key people have left because they only had 20 minutes. This is critically important to remember when you are preparing your demo and writing your script. Be sure to begin with the end and get your audience excited right out of the gate.

Pay attention to your audience

Let's carry this thought a half step further. When you do begin with the end and arrive at that first big 'ah-ha' moment, pay a great deal of attention to how the audience responds. This is presumably one of – if not THE – most impressive things that you plan to show during your demonstration. If it doesn't educe a positive response, then you may have an issue. If that is the case, we want to figure that out now and decide where to go from here, rather than continue down the planned path.

Pause for affect

How do we do this? Open with your finale, and then pause for a moment to give the audience a chance to digest what they've just seen. Let the significance or the importance of what you just showed them to sink in. In fact, I typically wait until I get a question or a comment. If we've done this right, and it's an impressive capability, there ought to be at least one comment or question from someone. If there isn't, then ask for some feedback. For example, *"What I just showed you was intended to be our precise answer to one of your key challenges. Do you see how what I just did satisfied that requirement?"* Don't move on until you get a response. This is a critical moment in the demo. If the audience isn't responding to this, chances are they aren't going to respond to anything else and we may have an expectation mismatch at this point.

The mistake that people make in this situation is that they sense that what they've just shown is not resonating with the audience. But instead of pausing and teasing that out, they get anxious and feel the natural tendency to explain more. When in fact they may be digging themselves a deeper hole.

So, pause. Allow time for feedback and questions. And tease it out if nothing comes naturally.

Explain but Don't Over-Explain

This is the perfect lead in for the next technique that we need to develop, and that is to *explain, but don't overexplain*. As we have said numerous times in this book, we're engineers by trade. We tend to come from technical backgrounds. And since we're in this role, more than likely we enjoy speaking to audiences. Add those two elements together and what do you get? People who like to explain things. It's what we do. It's how we're wired.

For certain, it's part of the role. It's our job to explain how things work. But we need to be careful not to overexplain things as we go. We do not need to explain every click. Remember this isn't training. It's presales. We do not need to point out every menu option, feature, button. A demo should not be a "grand tour" of the product. If someone asks about a specific feature or function, then of course provide an answer. But be careful not to go too deep into the weeds. If you do, you run the risk of boring the more senior team members in the room who likely have limited time and very little interest in (or patience for) diving into unnecessary levels of detail.

The other danger area for SEs where this principle is concerned is when something doesn't seem to resonate with the audience. If we show a key point and the audience doesn't respond the way we hope or expect, we tend to want to explain it more, in a different way. As if the audience just didn't understand the first time.

Problem is, chances are they either didn't understand you the first time – and now you're making things worse by going deeper, running the risk of confusing them more – or they weren't particularly impressed. In which case, going further may annoy them. In either case, trying to explain the point more is the wrong course of action.

How can I avoid this?

Good question. The trigger is repetition. If you find yourself repeating something over and over, in a different way, catch yourself. Pause and revert to a question. You can even say that very thing. *"I feel like I'm repeating myself here folks. Does this make sense, what I'm saying here? Are there any questions? I don't want to belabor the point."*

I'll practice what I'm preaching. You get the idea.

Don't Think Aloud

A related tip is to *avoid thinking aloud*. I challenge you to record one of your next web demos. Or sit through that of a colleague and listen for how many times either you or your colleague thinks aloud. It detracts so much from the delivery of a demo.

I'm sure you know what I'm referring to. The person giving the demo seems to have this running dialog with themselves, almost as if they are giving a play-by-play account of what they are doing. It sounds something like this.

> *"So, I'm going to move my mouse across the screen like so. I select the record I want. Then I click <open>. I see that the particular record is incomplete, so I'm going right click and select find child records..."*

NO! Please do not subject your audience to your mental streams of thought. This is so distracting. And so uninteresting to listen to. Make it interesting. Make it a story. If you must speak while moving the mouse, give "color commentary" instead of "play-by-play".

A better way to describe that same scenario might go something like this. *"I need to understand the status of this case and verify the data. So, let's take a look."* It's a totally different experience for the audience!

Don't Assume They Understand Your Terminology

The next important best practice to follow when you are presenting to a customer is to be careful with the terminology you use. This is another way in which we can lose or confuse our customers. We make the mistake of *assuming they understand our terminology.*

Let me assure you, in most cases, there are no bonus points for using high-tech, smart sounding words and terms if our audience doesn't understand them. Frankly, it makes us sound pompous and arrogant, and we run the risk of insulting them, in addition to confusing them.

Allow me to share a real-world example. I worked for a software company and one of the most compelling capabilities in the product was a mechanism called a "region". It was a rules engine that could be configured to display data-driven visual indicators. To be sure, the name was completely and totally misleading and confusing. Yet, in the early days of giving demos – before we implemented the best practices I'm talking about in this book – we would go to great lengths talking about *regions*, and what could be done with them, how powerful they were, etc.

I remember to this day, observing a demo by one of my colleagues and after about 10 minutes of listening to the power of *regions* and what they could be used for, the key stakeholder in the room raised his hand and said, *"I'm sorry, what's a region?"* The previous ten minutes of the demo were completely and totally lost on him, and we had to go back to the very beginning, to everyone's dismay.

Be sure not to lose people along the way with terminology that people outside your organization or industry may not understand. In fact, let's take this concept a half step further. During the technical discovery call, you should be listening for key terms that they use and weave *their* language into your demo, as much as possible.

Please Slow Down

The next technique to remember is to simply *slow down* and be deliberate. When you're giving a software demonstration, one of the primary goals is to make the tool to look easy. You want it to look simple, painless and easy to use.

Run your demo with as few mouse movements and clicks as possible. Minimize things like zooming in and zooming out. Minimize unnecessary mouse movements. I don't know why but for some reason, we have a tendency to feel like the mouse on the screen should be moving while we are speaking. It's just not true. In fact, it can be downright distracting. Unless you are clicking into something, or drawing specific attention to something, leave the mouse still. Say what you have to say. And then click into your next point.

As experts in our particular software, we tend to enjoy demonstrating our expertise in the tool. Typically, we can all navigate the pages and capabilities of the tool quickly, with ease. We get excited. We get amped up, especially if somebody asks a question that we have a particularly good answer for. We tend to get overly eager, moving from this screen to that. We will flow from one option to the next, one page to another, etc.

Problem is, we make the mistake of moving so fast that the audience can't keep up. They don't even know what they're seeing, much less where they've been.

Why is this a problem?

What we don't realize (or tend to forget) is that in attempt to make things look easy, navigating too fast can have the opposite effect. It can, in fact, make things look more complicated than they really are.

More importantly, we just confuse people. By clicking through the solution too quickly, we lose people along the way.

If there's a very specific thread, that showing the customer will help get to the technical win, take your time and be deliberate with the mouse and actions on the screen. Even if it requires multiple steps. You are better off taking your time than clicking through too quickly. This can be particularly true over the web.

A Confused Mind Always Says NO

The last few principles we have discussed: being cautious not to overexplain, avoiding terminology our customers may not understand and slowing ourselves down, are presented with one very specific goal in mind – to avoid confusing our audience. Because if there's anything I've learned over the years, a *confused mind always says NO*.

Allow me to repeat that again for emphasis. A confused mind always says no. Our goal – as we have discussed ad nauseam – is to get the technical win; to get the customer to say YES. However, if we confuse our audience along the way – even if they're impressed with what they see – the answer will be NO.

Please keep this in mind as you're giving your demonstrations. Not only do we want them to like us, like our product and the company; not only do we want them to see that our solution can help them meet their needs; we need to make sure that they understand what it is that we have demonstrated. We want to be sure not to confuse them along the way.

Know Your "Ah-Ha" Moments

Let's take this conversation a step further. As important as it is to avoid confusing our audiences, it is equally important to get our audiences excited. Excited for *what*? Excited for what's *possible*.

Excited for working with our product and our company. We want to create a vision for the future – one that includes using our software to make life easier. We do this by infusing enthusiasm into our demonstrations. We do this with *'Ah-Ha'* moments.

I've mentioned the 'Ah-Ha' moment a few times earlier in the book but haven't defined what it is. You can probably guess, but to make sure there's no confusion, allow me to do so now. The "ah-ha" moments in the demo are those screens, views, reports, etc. that when clicked into get "Ooh and Aahs" in response from the audience – almost as if they are watching fireworks. Or at least, they are supposed to.

Think of them as those moments in the demo in which you show an aspect of the solution that puts it all together – those moments where it all clicks into place for your audience. You almost quite literally want to see them saying to themselves, *"Ah-ha. Now I get it. Now I see how and why you're different."*

They are the moments, frankly, that make a demo a sales activity as opposed to a training activity. Demos should be built around the *ah-ha* moments. There should be 3-5 such moments in most demos, explicitly planted at optimal times. One of which – in fact the biggest of which – should be in the first 2-5 minutes of the demo. (We covered that in the section *Begin with the End*.) Everything else is setup and brief explanation. Any more than 3-5 *ah-ha* moments and the demo has the potential to become overwhelming. Anything less, and your demo probably is just a grand tour through the tool with too little sizzle.

When you are giving your demonstration, be sure to know where those moments are; when they are coming. Use them to your advantage. Be sure to have everyone's attention. Be sure the key people are in the room. Be sure to set them up by describing the problem and elaborating the symptoms. The ideal situation is to bring the audience to the edge of their seat a little bit. Get them intrigued. Pique their curiosity. And then click, unveil the solution, the answer, the "Wow".

Pause and Let It Sink In

When you do reach one of your ah-ha moments, remember to *pause and let it sink in*. I mentioned this earlier, and I'll repeat it here for emphasis, because it's so important during a software demonstration. Fear not the momentary pause – especially after you've delivered one of your ah-ha moments.

The mistake that so many SEs make is they click into one of the more compelling views or capabilities of the tool, but then hardly come up for air. They move on to their next point so quickly that the audience hardly has a moment to digest what they've just seen. In many cases the audience misses the point altogether or wrongly makes the assumption that it wasn't all that important.

Know where your 'ah-ha' moments are. Build up as much intrigue and interest as you can leading up to them. Then pause afterwards for emphasis and let them sink in.

What if it doesn't sink in?

Hhmmm. Good question. What *if* the ah-ha moment doesn't sink in? Doesn't seem to resonate with the audience or educe the response you were expecting? Stop and ask!

> *"Did you follow what I just did there folks? That was one of the more important capabilities that we wanted to share with you today. Did you understand the significance of what I just showed you?"*

The worst thing you can do – and I've seen it dozens of times – is to present one of your *ah-ha* moments, have it fall flat, and then, rather than pause and take the temperature of the room, barrel ahead with the demo, hoping that talking more and showing more will get the room more excited. Wrong!

This is so important in the context of a demo. If you just showed something that was supposed to be one of the more impressive capabilities of your platform – a feature that makes your product unique or specifically addresses one of their requirements. This should be one of the more poignant moments in your demo. If they don't respond, do not forge ahead. If they didn't like *that*, chances are they aren't going to like what's next. Stop and figure out why. Did they not understand? Were they not impressed? Did it not work the way they were expecting? Maybe they are just unsure, and they're reserving judgment until it's over. That's OK too. But as an SE, we want to know where our audience is mentally, before we continue.

Be Yourself

It is said that audiences tend to remember the first and last thing a speaker says. I wonder if the same is true for any given chapter of a book. I toyed with making this principle the first in this chapter. But, as you can clearly see, I decided to end with it. It's because violating this one important principle undermines all the benefits of applying the other rules. It's the foundation upon which all the others are based. Simply put, when you give a demonstration, no matter what, *be yourself*.

As the very name of this chapter suggests – PERFORM – I do think of a software demonstration as a performance. I believe any time we stand in front of a professional audience – whether it's giving a software demonstration, running a training class, or speaking at a conference, etc. – there's an element of being a performer. We have to be "on".

I think some people may be uncomfortable with this idea – that a software demonstration is a *performance*. It may be perceived as "putting on a show" or "putting on an act", which may have the connotation of being false or fake. That's *not* what's being suggested here in the least. Quite the contrary. Nothing could be further from the truth. To perform at your best in this role you need to be yourself. You need to be *authentic*. Do *not* try to be someone else. *That* would be fake.

Many people in this profession – by the very nature of the job – are outgoing, talkative, love to be in front of an audience, etc. But not everyone. And it is not a requirement. In fact, some of the best SEs I've had the privilege of working with and seeing in action, are very low key and reserved. They know it, and they own it.

To be successful in this role; to perform at your best in front of an audience, be yourself. If you're more low-key than some, or have a dry sense of humor, build that into your delivery. If you're outgoing and gregarious, use that to your advantage. Whatever your style is, know it and own it.

With self-awareness, however, comes the opportunity to self-govern as well. If you know that you have the tendency to be an "over-the-top" extrovert, and you are meeting with a group of engineers who seem to be a little more socially reserved, you might want to tone it down a little for this group. Likewise, if your style is more reserved and you're meeting with a group of outgoing extroverts from a marketing agency, for example, you might want to try to step up your energy a little. Regardless of the situation, at the end of the day, the best advice I can give to anyone in the role is to be authentic. Be yourself.

CHAPTER 7

HABIT #5 – PERFORM (PART 2)

Getting the Technical Win

In the first two segments of Habit #5 – PERFORM, we covered the techniques necessary to a) effectively "tee up" the demo, and b) deliver a compelling and engaging demo. We will now turn our attention to getting the *technical win*. We've talked a lot about that throughout the book. However, the techniques presented in this chapter will equip you to move from effective delivery to close. Everything we've said and done up until now has positioned us for the technical win. Now it's time to cross the finish line.

How to Answer Questions

The first topic we're going to cover is how to answer questions – specifically how to most effectively answer questions in such a way that we produce, even drive the result we're looking for.

INSIGHT: *I've come to believe that the ability to answer questions effectively may very well be the most important skill we can develop. I believe the way in which we respond to questions has the greatest impact on winning or losing the deal.*

Why is this so important?

Because going into any demonstration we know what it is that *we* are going to say. Assuming we've done our homework. Assuming we've followed the guidance provided in this book – the partnership is in good standing, we've probed into the customer's request, we've prepared effectively, and we've practiced to verify that everything is working. As a result, we should feel pretty good going in and have a reasonably good idea of what to expect.

Fact is, we have a fair amount of control over what we're going to say and do. What do we not have control over? What is it that's most difficult to anticipate? The *questions* we are going to be asked. We have no control over what we are going to be asked, in what context, by whom, and when. From my experience, it is how you handle those questions – how you respond to and address those questions – that will ultimately determine your success. Let's pick this apart a little.

Expect Questions

To begin with, we need to go into demos *expecting questions*. The first mistake that SEs make in this context is they sometimes almost act surprised when a question is asked. Or worse they act offended, as if to say, "What, do you not understand what I just showed you? Did you not just hear me?" "Are you questioning or challenging *me*?"

Rule number one is to enter demonstrations expecting to receive questions from the audience and be prepared to answer them.

Let's go a step further. You should be looking for questions; *hoping* for questions. No company has ever spent money on software without first asking questions – lots of them. In fact, I'm not sure anyone has ever bought anything of any real value without first doing their due diligence and asking lots of questions. It's quite simple. If you're audience isn't asking questions, they will not be buying your software. They either don't understand, or worse, they don't care. Either way, no questions is a bad sign.

No Question is a Bad Question

I know it's a cliché. But in a sales demonstration, it holds very true. There's no such thing as a bad question. Why?

Because every question is an *insight*. It's an insight into what this individual is thinking. It's an insight into what the group may be thinking or what their concerns are. It may be an insight into how well informed or educated this individual is. It may be an insight into whether this person is a "friend or foe." It may be an insight into where this individual ranks on the team. Whatever the case may be, treat every question as an opportunity to gain an insight – into the individual and into the team.

Pay attention not only to the question, but to the context of the question – the motivation behind the question. Ask yourself not only *what* the person is asking, but *why* is this person asking what they're asking. Are they sincerely trying to understand your product and how it works? Are they trying to make a point of their own? Are they challenging you or trying to expose a weakness in your solution? Does their question indicate that they don't understand something that you've already covered? Does their question indicate that they don't seem to be in sync with others on the team? Etc. Etc. I could go on and on.

The point is, every question is an offering. It's an offering of information that you can use to help drive and steer the conversation. It's critically important to do this before you craft a response because the context and the motivation behind the question should influence how you respond.

Acknowledge the question and the person who asked

So, we know to be looking for questions – in fact, hoping for questions. We understand that every question offers insights. How should we handle questions? What is the best way to respond?

To begin with, as a best practice, the first thing you should almost always do is 1) acknowledge the *question*, and 2) acknowledge the *person* asking the question – and do so by using the person's name. Even if the question seems irrelevant or ill-intended, it is important to do these two things.

Allow me to give you an example. You receive a question from one of the attendees in the room. Your first response might be, *"Good question Bob. Glad you asked."* Or *"Excellent question Mary. I think I see where you're going with that line of thought."* What are we doing there? We're acknowledging the question and giving recognition to the person.

What if I've forgotten the person's name?

Just ask! *"Oh. Good question. So glad you asked. I'm sorry, remind me your name. Right, Bob. Glad you asked. Let's take a closer look at that."* This makes the meeting more conversational. It makes it more engaging. We are on a first name basis now. It's almost like we're becoming friends. People will begin to warm up to you, and they may not even know why.

---

*INSIGHT: There is such a thing as "too much of a good thing" where this is concerned. Something I learned the hard way is that it **is** possible to go overboard. I recall a demonstration – a long, 2-hour demonstration and meeting – during which I was asked dozens of questions. It's very natural for me to respond with "Good question. I'm glad you asked." Or "Excellent question. Let's pick that apart." And during this meeting, I did this constantly – throughout the entire meeting. A few weeks later, I was chatting with one of the attendees* *after they had become customers. We were talking about the demo I had given a few weeks back. She thought it was a good demo, but she said that I was beginning to sound disingenuous because I responded to every question with "Good question," "Great question," etc. Her advice to me was to use that response a little more sparingly. That's now my advice to others like you. Be polite. Acknowledge both the question and the individual. But do so judiciously. Don't lay it on so thick that it begins to sound insincere.*

Repeat the Question

What you do next is another key step in the process of effectively handling questions. *Repeat the question!* This is so powerful, and yet so few of us use this secret. (Our sales counterparts could probably benefit from learning this one as well.) When you get a question – especially a tough question that may take a moment or two to think about – once you have acknowledged the question and the person, simply repeat the question. Why? There are a couple of reasons this is so powerful.

Number one, it's your opportunity to clarify that you do in fact understand the question – for your sake and for theirs. How many times have you seen an SE – heck, anyone for that matter – provide an answer to a question they *thought* they heard, discover after a long-winded answer that they misunderstand the question?

Why is this such a big problem in the context of a demo? At the very least, we may be wasting the little precious time we have with the customer. We may annoy them with our inability to understand what they are saying. In fact, it may make us look a little less intelligent or intuitive. But worse, by answering a question we thought we heard but wasn't asked, we may expose a weakness of the tool unnecessarily! Yikes! We don't want to do that!

By repeating the question, it gives us the opportunity to verify and clarify the question. The dialog may go something like this: Customer asks a question. You respond with, *"Good question Bob.*

I'm glad you asked. Just so I'm clear, I think what you're asking is..."
And then you restate the question IN YOUR OWN WORDS. (Please
do not restate the question in the same, exact words. That would be
insulting.)

At this point, upon hearing his question restated, he is likely to do
one of three things.

1. He may further clarify and ask an even more specific question.
   Which is very good for us because the narrower the question,
   the easier it is to answer.

2. He may say, *"No. You misunderstood me. What I'm really asking
   is..."* and then he'll ask his own question again, only this time in
   a different way so that it's clearer. To which, you can again
   respond with, *"Ah. OK. So, what you're really asking is..."* Now
   you have a much better understanding of what's being asked.

3. Upon hearing his own question restated back to him, he may
   tell you to disregard. He may realize it's not all that important,
   or maybe he's answered the question on his own. In fact, one of
   his colleagues may even chime in at that point and suggest that
   the question isn't overly relevant and can wait.

Whatever the case, all three of these outcomes are good for us. It
puts us in a better position to answer the question effectively or not
have to at all.

One of the most common mistakes that SEs make, is they get so
used to hearing the same questions over and over, that they start
anticipating specific questions. Or they hear a question that they
think they have a great answer for. They'll start answering some
questions before the person asking has even gotten the words out.
The problem with this is that it's rude to begin with, but more
importantly we run the risk of assuming the wrong question,
hearing the wrong question, and as such, answering the wrong
question.

Taking this approach forces us to pause, listen to the entire question, and repeat the question for clarity, preventing us from interrupting and getting it wrong.

Buy yourself some time

Restating the question does one other thing for us as well. It buys us some time. It gives us 30-60 seconds or more to consider how we might go about answering the question. This is particularly important if the question being asked is a tough one to answer. When you find yourself in this situation – someone has asked you a tough question. Restate the question, then immediately begin to think about the answer. The person might rephrase the question, making it easier to answer, or decide that it's a question that can wait. But if they don't, you've at least given yourself a minute to think about the best way to respond.

Do I really need to go through this whole process every time?

The answer is a resounding NO. There is no need to go to this extent with every question. Use your best judgment. Some questions may be very simple and straightforward, and can be answered with a simple yes or no. Refer to the previous chapter in which we discussed the "check down" method for answering questions and the *3Vs* – first give a *verbal* response, then show *visual* evidence, then go into *vivid* detail, but only if necessary.

Question is, how do we determine when it is appropriate and necessary to go deep and address a question head on? That is an important question, for which we need to make one more key distinction.

All Questions Are Not Created Equally

Over the years and after the hundreds of demos I've both given and observed, there is one truism that I have come to know beyond a fraction of a doubt. In the context of a software demo, all questions *are not created equally*. What do I mean by that? Some questions are completely and totally irrelevant, as far as the success of the software deal is concerned. However, in stark contrast to that, there will always be key questions, asked by key individuals, at key moments, that make or break the deal.

The challenge that we, as sales engineers face, is recognizing questions accordingly and knowing how to handle them, multiple times in any demo, on the fly, in front of an audience. That's pressure. For that, we need a system. We need a process.

Assess the Person. Assess the Question

Allow me to introduce to you a simple two-step process you can quickly use to determine, on the fly, the best way to handle any difficult question in any given demonstration.

1. **Assess the person asking the question.**
    Are they critical or central to the decision-making process or on the "periphery"? In other words, are they a *key player* or a *non-key player*?

2. **Assess the question being asked.**
    Is it pertinent to the agreed upon scope and requirements, or irrelevant and unrelated? That is, is the question *on-topic* or *off-topic*?

The answers to these two questions will dictate how we handle questions from the audience. They should dictate how you respond and to what extent.

Consider a matrix in which the vertical axis represents the first question – regarding the person – and the horizontal axis represents the second – regarding the question itself. The matrix is organized into four quadrants. (See chart below.)

When asked a question that you sense has the potential to be a little tricky or complex, you need to make a very quick assessment according to the model and respond accordingly.

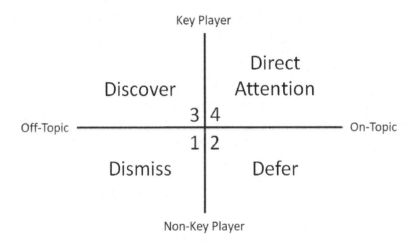

Figure 7: Demo Q&A Matrix. The "Four D's"

Quadrant 1

The lower left-hand corner, *Quadrant 1*, represents those questions that have been asked by a *non-key player* – maybe someone who was invited to attend the meeting at the last minute, and their question is *off topic* and outside of the agreed upon scope, which as you recall, we should have established up front. In most cases, we want to *DISMISS* this question, as quickly and as politely as possible.

Follow our rules: Acknowledge the person. Acknowledge the question. Repeat the question, if appropriate. Then turn to one of the more key members of the team and ask for clarity or guidance.

Your response might sound something like this. *"Thanks for your question Mary. Interesting point you've raised."* Then, looking at one of the team leads, *"Tom, I don't recall this being one of your requirements. Is this something we need to include?"* Chances are Tom (in this example) will turn to Mary and ask her to keep those questions to herself, as they aren't pertinent to the conversation at hand, or something of that nature. Question dismissed; we can continue down our path.

The mistake that SEs make in this category is they spend unnecessary time answering questions asked by people who aren't close to or involved in the deal and, as such, aren't pertinent to the conversation. From my experience, your audience will appreciate the fact that you didn't waste anyone's time addressing a question that had no direct bearing on the discussion at hand. They will also respect you for handling it with courtesy and finesse. In this regard, you're actually building credibility and rapport with the people who DO matter as far as the opportunity is concerned.

Quadrant 2

The lower right-hand corner, *Quadrant 2*, represents those questions that have been asked by a *non-key player* but are *on-topic*. If you can quickly and easily answer the question, then do so. However, I often find that these questions are asked at inappropriate times. If you know you're going to address that question later in the demo, the best response may be to *DEFER* the question until later, so as to not disrupt your demo flow. Again, you will likely find that the audience is appreciative that you stayed on course and didn't redirect based on a question from someone who's not part of the core team.

The mistake that SEs make here is they derail the demo, unnecessarily for something they are going to cover anyways – often times to their own detriment. Unless it's a key player asking the question, stay on course.

Quadrant 3

The upper left-hand corner, Quadrant 3, represents those questions that have been asked by a *key-player*, but the question is *off topic* and outside the scope of what's been agreed to that day. This is arguably the most challenging scenario. We're dealing with a key player here. It's important that we answer their questions – to their satisfaction. But the question being asked is off topic. It might even seem irrelevant. It might feel like you're being thrown a curveball. When you get a question like this, what should you do?

Immediately drop into *DISCOVERY* mode. In fact, act surprised – maybe even a little confused. State that this seems to be a new requirement, and you don't recall this coming up before. Also – and this is key – ask how important this new requirement is.

It might sound something like this. *"Oh. Interesting question Linda. I don't recall this coming up before. Is this a new requirement? Is this something you need to be able to see in our platform? How important is this in the context of everything else we've talked about thus far?"*

With that they might tell you to disregard the question. That it was only a fleeting thought and they were just curious. Or you might discover that, yes, in fact, it is something that is important and something that needs to be addressed – either in your demo or by the platform, etc. Now you have a choice to make. Is it something you address then, in real time? If so, shift gears, turn, pivot and address the question in real time. This is, after all, a key player, and he/she may have to leave in 5-10 minutes.

Maybe it's something you need to defer to a later date. If so, simply explain that you are unprepared to include it in the demonstration in that moment but will be happy to reconvene. One of the worst things we can do when confronted with a question like this is to attempt to give some BS answer that the individual will likely see right through. Or show something half-baked and unprepared. If you're unprepared to address the question, say so and defer it to later, but only after you've done some discovery.

Quadrant 4

The upper right-hand corner, *Quadrant 4*, represents those questions that have been asked by a *key player*, and the question is *on topic*. The one thing you want to be sure to do is *DIRECT* all your attention to this question, and answer it to his/her satisfaction, right away.

This may seem obvious, but the mistake SEs make is they'll treat questions in this quadrant like they would questions that fall into Quadrant 2 – questions asked by non-key players. If the question being asked is something we're going to address later in the demo, we may be tempted to defer the individual until later. But in doing so, what have we just done? We've indicated that our agenda – our "precious demo script" – is more important to us than their question.

If this is a high-ranking employee of the company or member of the team, they may be very offended. They probably aren't used to being told to hold their question until later – especially not by a lowly engineer. What's worse is they may be asking because they know they have to leave the meeting early and are sincerely interested in one specific thing. So, not only have we possibly insulted this individual, but they may no longer be in the room when you do get to it.

It's quite simple. If you get a question from a key player in the deal, and it's on topic and in scope, direct all your attention to that person and that question, and do everything you can to address the question to their satisfaction right then and there.

Answering Questions – In a Nutshell

That concludes the section on questions and how to answer them. When answered properly, appropriately, and to your customer's satisfaction, they will win you deals. When answered or handled poorly, they may very well be the reason you lose.

To summarize how to handle questions here is the list of rules we covered.

1. Go into every demo expecting questions – looking for questions
2. No question is a bad question – they offer insights
3. Pay attention to the context of the question – look for hidden agendas
4. Acknowledge the question
5. Acknowledge the person – by name
6. Do so judiciously
7. Repeat the question
8. Assess the person asking the question – key player or non-key player
9. Assess the question itself – on-topic or off-topic
10. Respond accordingly – Dismiss, Defer, Discover, Direct Attention

Crafting Your Responses

Now that we have addressed how to handle questions, let's spend a moment discussing some specifics around how to craft your responses. Remember, we are in sales. We use different language in presales conversations than we do in post-sales conversations. Leverage these techniques to drastically improve your success rate in sales engagements.

Don't be Afraid to Say "I Don't Know"

The most effective SEs know their boundaries. They know when they've gone "above their technical pay grade," as I like to say. They also recognize that it's unrealistic for anyone to be expected to know everything. There is no shame in saying to a customer *'I don't know.'* When you are asked a question that you sincerely do not know the answer to, simply acknowledge the question and explain that it's beyond your area of expertise.

Not only is it the right thing to do, it will help build credibility and rapport. Admitting that you don't know something makes you more human. It also shows your audience you will give them an honest answer. One of the worst things you can do is fabricate a BS answer on the fly. It's usually transparent when we do, and it tends to come off as disingenuous.

It's ok to offer an "educated guess" or a hunch, if you have a relatively good one. But be sure to let them know that that's what it is – a hunch and not a definitive answer. Explain to them that you are not the expert in that area, but you can offer your understanding. Responding with a guess that sounds like a fact has the potential to be misleading and may damage the sale. We do not want to lose credibility with our customer.

Regardless of how you respond, if it's something you're not sure of, always offer to take it as an action item – something you will research. It shows that you want to be sure that all their questions are answered. And, more importantly, it gives you a reason to have another conversation, which is always a good thing.

Learn to Say No Without Using the Word NO

Rarely in a software demonstration – aka sales conversation – is the answer to any question an absolute, binary yes or no. In virtually all cases, there is some grey area for just about every response. To that end, one of the skills that high performing SEs develop is the ability to say no without using the word "no." When they get a question to which the answer may seem to be no on the surface, they will either qualify the question, or they will offer a "qualified yes."

Qualify the Question

Let's say the customer asks, *"Does your platform offer version control?"* On the surface, the quick and easy answer may be no. But how do you know exactly what the customer means by "version control?" Is it possible that what their definition of version control is something the tool can in fact support? Is it possible that there is a combination of things that the tool does that could be considered "version control," in their minds?

In this situation, the skilled SE might respond with, *"Good question. We hear this often. Before I explain version control, help me understand what you mean by version control. What are the specific things you are looking for in this context?"* By responding this way, you are asking them to clarify and specify their question. This will give you the opportunity to provide a much better answer, and hopefully, ultimately respond with a "yes and this is how."

It's uncanny, frankly, how often the answer to a question goes from no to yes, ONCE the question has been specified and clarified. So rather than opening with "no" and risk closing the door on that conversation, qualify the question first to see if you can uncover a "yes."

Below are a few examples of how you might get deeper into the question. Going back to the "version control" example...

- *"Different organizations think of version control in different ways. How do you define version control?"*
- *"The answer may be yes or no depending on the specifics of what you are looking for."*
- *"To what extent are you looking for version control?"*

Provide a Qualified Yes

What does it mean to provide a *qualified yes*? Again, rarely are answers to questions in a demo binary, i.e. "yes or no". A mistake that SEs make is they lean towards "No" first, and then qualify the no with a set of conditions and exceptions, within which the answer would be "Yes." Those that do this tend to argue that they are giving an honest answer. NO! No, no, no! This is *not* just being honest. It's being *cautious*. It's being *defensive*. It's being overly concerned about *your* credibility. And frankly, putting yourself ahead of the deal. Remember, our goal is to get the technical win for the benefit of the team.

What I'm suggesting here is that we turn that model on its head. Rather than responding with NO and then qualifying it. Respond with YES, and then qualify it. It's the SAME THING, only in a more positive light.

Let's go back to the example we used a moment ago, "Does your tool support version control?" A negative response or "closed door" response, might be something like *"No, not really, unless you consider XYZ to be version control."* (By the way, maybe they DO consider that version control. That's why we need to start there in the first place!)

A more positive, open-minded response would look like this. *"In fact, yes it does. Maybe not exactly in the way you're thinking about version control, but there's certainly version control built in. Allow me to explain."* And if that sounds too over the top, use a softer tone like this, *"Well there is version control, but it may be different than what you have in mind. Help me understand what you're looking for."*

This sounds like "Spin" to me

Some people might call this spin. Some people might even consider this misleading. I disagree. In my mind, this is putting our best foot forward. Remember, we're in sales. Sales is a courtship. It is our job to present our software in the best light possible.

Another way to respond might be to offer a work-around or a customization. *"It's not something we do natively"* or *"it's not an out-of-the-box capability, but it's certainly something that can be configured or customized,"* etc. Again, it's saying no in a more positive way.

INSIGHT: *I feel pretty strongly about this point (in case it's not obvious). If you sincerely feel uncomfortable about this idea of responding with a 'qualified yes', I would seriously evaluate the decision to be in this line of work. To me, this is one of the big differences between being in presales and post-sales roles. At the very least I would encourage you to take this section of the book and share it with your SE manager and/or sales counterparts and have a discussion on the topic. I would be shocked if they didn't share my perspective on this to some degree.*

Even if the customer is asking a question to which the answer is an almost certain no, we still don't need to respond with a direct "no." Going back to the version control example, we might say, *"Version control? Hmmm... Unfortunately, I'm not sure. I don't think so. Not the way you're probably thinking. Can you help me understand what it is that you're thinking? Maybe it's a requirement we can bring to the product team."* The point is, this is still more open-minded and conversational than a direct *"No it doesn't do that,"* which just comes off close-minded and rigid.

Can you share a real-life example of this?

I'd be delighted to. I attended a demo recently and the topic was application security. We were presenting to a reasonably large group of folks that we had not previously met with before. It was a web demonstration, so it was very hard to tell how engaged the audience was. Unfortunately, there was very little interaction. We were about two thirds into the presentation and demo – which was largely one-sided – and finally someone on the phone spoke up. It was one of the more senior folks from the team. She asked, *"Does your software provide threat analysis?"* How did the SE respond? *"No. It doesn't."* And then he continued with the demo without missing a beat!

What a missed opportunity! We hadn't hardly heard a word from anyone on the phone up until that point. It was our first opportunity to get the audience engaged. Although the SE in this case was technically correct. The software wasn't formally positioned in the "threat analysis" space. It's quite possible that someone might consider what the software did as being a threat analysis capability on some level. It would depend on their definition or interpretation of threat analysis. And how do we know if we don't ask?

The worst part of it, in this particular case, was that it was finally an opportunity to engage the attendees in some dialogue. They had hardly said a word up until that moment. We could have responded with, *"Good question. I'm glad you asked. Help me understand how you define threat analysis. We might not support it in the way you are thinking, but customers certainly use our software to minimize security risk. So, the answer might be yes."*

This is the difference between simply answering questions and using questions to begin a dialogue. We are not there to just answer technical questions. We are there to engage our customers in conversations – sales conversations.

Are you suggesting it's OK to lie to a prospect?

By no means, in the least, am I suggesting that you lie or mislead your audience, quite the contrary. I tell the people I work with, and I'm telling you here now, we *always* tell the truth. It's the right thing to do. It's good business. And, if we don't, it will only hurt us and our customers in the long run.

But telling the truth doesn't have to be negative. Telling the truth can be done in a positive, optimistic, solution-oriented manner. That's all I'm suggesting here. Let's lead with "yes" answers and qualify them down, as opposed to leading with "no" answers and qualify them up.

Is there EVER a time we should say NO?

Great question! Yes! Read on.

The Power of Saying NO

You may be asking yourself this question. *"Is there EVER a time we should respond with a direct no?"* The answer is yes – a resounding yes at that. And for reasons which may surprise you. In fact, it might even seem a bit contradictory to what we just discussed in the previous section on giving a qualified yes but follow me here. There is *POWER in saying a direct NO* – at least once in every demo. Let's take a closer look.

As you go through your demo, and you make your way through the questions and answers, restating them, seeking clarification, plotting them in our matrix, etc., you will very likely find yourself facing a question that is very specific and very direct to which the answer is a definitive no. When you find yourself in that situation, look your audience straight in the eye and say, with confidence and a touch of empathy, *"No. I'm sorry. The tool doesn't do that."*

It's powerful! Why? Because you have now just validated every single answer you have provided up until that point. Your audience now knows that if the answer to any one of their questions is a sincere and definitive no, you will give it to them straight.

Are you saying I should go out of my way to say no?

No. That's not what I'm saying here at all. This is not a technique to manipulate your audience. Please don't abuse this. Chances are you may quite happily go through an entire demo and not have a single opportunity to respond with a direct no. And that's not necessarily an indication of how well the demo went. It just means the opportunity didn't present itself. But if there is an opportunity to respond with a direct no, then do so. It can be powerful.

Two Important Caveats

1. The question being asked should be relatively harmless to the deal, meaning it should be a trivial question or a non-critical requirement – something that is very unlikely to derail the deal. Going back to our matrix, we should NOT be responding with a direct no to a question in Quadrant 4 – something being asked by a key person related to a point that's in scope, unless it is a minor specification. So be cautious here.
2. You should always follow your "no" response immediately with a qualifying question. *"Is that going to be a problem?"* Since we opted to give the direct no response, we should be reasonably certain that it isn't a problem. But we want to confirm right then and there that it isn't a problem. We also want everyone in the room to hear right then and there, that it isn't going to be a problem. We don't want it to become something they use downstream against us in negotiations or as an objection. And in the unlikely event it IS a problem, we want to know that right now too, so we can deal with it head on.

Let's return to our version control example. We asked for clarification, and it turns out our software does not provide version control the way they have asked. We sense it probably is not a critical issue. So, we think this is a safe and proper time to leverage the power of a direct no. *"No. I'm sorry. The tool doesn't support version control the way you have described it. Is that going to be a problem?"*

Put it on the table right then and there. If it is going to be a problem, we will find out now and can address it. If it's not – which we're hoping – everyone in the room now knows it too. It won't be used against us in future discussions.

Have you ever seen this backfire?

Good question. I'm reminded of a demonstration I attended as the senior member of the sales team, on site with a government customer several years ago. The SE had been through my training and was well versed in the "Power of Saying No." With me in the room, I had a feeling he was trying to implement as many of my tips and techniques as he could. And by the way, he was doing a great job. However, at one point during the meeting, there was a broad, reasonably open-ended question that came from arguably the most important person in the room – clearly a key player. Without missing a beat – and I'm sure taking a page from the training he had recently attended – he looked the gentleman straight on and said, "No. I'm sorry. The software doesn't do that."

I almost swallowed my teeth. Yes, I believe in the power of saying no, but not necessarily to the most important guy, early in a demo, in response to a broad question that left lots of room for interpretation. That response momentarily sucked the air out of the room, and it took us a while to regain some momentum.

The lesson here is to be sure to use "The Power of Saying No" surgically and judiciously, or else it might backfire on you. It should be a very specific question on a non-central theme. If the answer to a broad question, asked by a key member of the decision-making team, that is central and relevant to the discussion at hand, is a definitive no, then we have not done a very good job of qualifying this opportunity, and we probably shouldn't be there to begin with.

Seek Feedback Along the Way

In the previous section, I shared a story about a question that was received during a demo about two thirds of the way in. It was the first question asked in almost 40 minutes of presentation and demo! How is that even possible? Why does that happen?

It turns out there are a variety of reasons for this. Some groups are just reluctant to ask questions. They may not want to interrupt your flow. It may be that they don't understand. There may be odd group dynamics in the room that make it uncomfortable to ask questions. There is a long list of reasons why your audience may not be engaged.

As SEs, it is our responsibility to create an environment in which comments and questions are welcomed and encouraged. It is our responsibility to draw our audiences out and discover what they like and don't like. We do this throughout our demonstrations by *constantly seeking feedback along the way.*

We have spent a lot of time talking about questions in this chapter. If your audience is engaged, and you are getting questions throughout your demo, then you may not need to proactively seek feedback. Consider yourself fortunate to have such an engaged, interested audience, and give yourself a pat on the back for drawing them out naturally.

However, if you find yourself speaking for 3-5 minutes without any questions or comments, get to a good breaking point, pause, and ask the audience an engaging question. You might say something simple like, *"That was a key point. Did you follow that?" "Before I go on, are there any questions about what I just showed?"* Ask something to get your audience engaged and involved.

More importantly, ask a question that will draw out some *insight*.

What is it that we want to know as we're going through our demos?

1. Do they understand what they are seeing?
2. Do they like what they are seeing?
3. Do they have any questions about what they are seeing?

The answers to these questions should constantly be in your mind. They should constantly be steering you and the direction of your demo.

Make it Conversational

When you do stop and ask for feedback, be sure to make it conversational and not robotic. Asking the question, "Does that make sense?" repeatedly, is not conversational. It's monotonous and boring. Below is a list of questions you can use to make a demo seem more conversational and interesting. Use a combination of these to keep the presentation fresh.

1. Are there any questions on what I just showed?
2. That was an important point. Did everyone get the significance of that?
3. I want to be sure I didn't go through that too fast. Did everyone follow that?
4. Allow me to pause. I just covered a lot of ground. Any questions?
5. This is an important point. I want to be sure this is clear to everyone before I press on.

I'm sure you get the point. Seek feedback along the way, but do so in a creative, engaging manner. Asking your audience, *"Does that make sense?"* every few minutes is not the way to endear yourself to your audience.

What if I don't get any responses?

That's OK. The reality is, it won't always work. You may be in a tough environment. You may struggle to draw the audience out, even with effective, engaging questions – for reasons that are beyond your control. Pay close attention to body language. Is your audience engaged? Are they paying attention? Do they look interested?

If you are not getting any questions and/or the audience doesn't appear to be engaged, it makes little sense to forge ahead with your demo. Look to one of the more senior members of the team or look to the person that hosted the meeting and address that person directly. *"I don't seem to be getting a lot of feedback yet. Is this in line with what you were expecting? Do you have any questions about we've covered so far?"* What we want to avoid is talking for too long without getting any feedback at all.

Does the number of people in the room matter?

Yes! The larger the group, the less inclined people are to speak. If you find yourself in a situation like that, and people aren't speaking up, fact is, the demo may be going very well. The attendees may just be reluctant to speak because of the large group. I still encourage you to attempt to try to draw people out by addressing one of the key players in the room.

Consider the Opposite

What's the opposite of this rule – *seek feedback along the way*? What's the mistake SEs make? They focus too much on their demo – their script. They start talking and clicking and ramble through the demo, unaware of the audience and body language in the room. They don't pause and ask for feedback. They talk for 15, 20, 25 minutes without coming up for air.

The audience may be confused, bored or disengaged, and the SE isn't even aware. Yes, this may be an extreme example. (And I'm certain none of you would make this mistake.) But I go to this length to emphasize the point. Seek feedback along the way. Stay tuned in to where your audience is and bring them along for the ride.

I'm a little uncomfortable with this – seek feedback

You might be uncomfortable with this – drawing people out. You might feel like you're prying or pressuring your audience. Admittedly, this does take some practice. And it takes some finesse. We don't want to come off like a high-pressure salesperson here. But we aren't in the business of giving lectures either. Those people are called teachers, which we are not. We are there for the audience's benefit. We are there to help them understand what our technology can do, how it can solve their problems and help them meet their objectives. We are there to help them make an informed purchase decision. How can we do that if we're not plugged in to what they're thinking? Of course, we are there for our company's benefit, as well – and our own. But it's our duty to help our customers make a good decision, and we can only do that if we get them engaged in the conversation.

The Mini-Close

We talked extensively in Chapter 2 about our role vs. that of our sales counterparts. We established that we are responsible for the technical win, and they are ultimately responsible for revenue, i.e. closing the deal. To that end, there's a technique we can use to subtly and gently move our audience closer to the technical win and help our sales counterparts close the deal faster, with fewer roadblocks. That technique is referred to as the *mini-close*.

What's a "mini-close"?

At face value, the mini-close looks a lot like a form of *seeking feedback*. It comes in the context of a question and is designed to get a response from the customer. However, what differentiates a mini-close from the questions we use to get the customer engaged is they are asked in such a way that require the customer to acknowledge, on some small level, that we've satisfied one of their requirements. What we are looking for with a mini-close is some level of commitment, if only in the very smallest measure. We are looking for a small step towards achieving the technical win.

How does this work?

Allow me to explain. If at some point in your demo you ask the following question, *"That was an important point. Did everyone get the significance of that?"* This is clearly an attempt to seek feedback and draw the audience into the conversation – which is a good thing. However, let's say, for argument's sake, you've had good engagement in the room. Your audience has been asking lots of questions. They seem to understand what you're showing them, and they seem impressed. This might be a good time for a *mini-close* to see just how far along they really are and whether you can "check that box", so to speak.

The mini-close version of that very same question might sound something more like this. *"Now that we've covered that part of the demo, do you see how that will satisfy your requirement in this area?"* Or *"It seems like this is resonating with you, can you see how you might use this in your organization to address that challenge?"*

What have we done here with the newer version – the "mini-close" version – of the question? We've taken it up a notch. We've gone from *"do you understand"* and *"are there any questions"* to *"are you satisfied"* and *"could see yourself using?"* On a very small level, we're asking for acknowledgement that we've satisfied a requirement. We're not asking for a commitment. We're not asking for a PO. We're just giving them a gentle nudge. We're trying to proactively take one small step towards the technical win.

Another flavor of the "mini-close" is to ask a question designed to make the solution seem that much more real in their minds. You might ask *"Now that you understand how this works, could you imagine yourself using this in your environment to address that issue?"* This is an incredibly effective way to ask the question, because not only are we looking for acknowledgement, but by design, we're asking them to imagine using the software in their day to day business.

Sounds to me like we're pressuring them

I had a feeling some of you might say that. In fact, some of you may be thinking this sounds like a high-pressure sales tactic. To be clear, yes, we are indeed applying a *little* bit of pressure. But that's it, just a little bit. And we only do this when we sense that we have some momentum in the room, that we're getting some buy-in to what we are showing. This is a "strike while the iron's hot" mentality.

So, timing is important here?

Yes! Timing is critical with regards to the mini-close. Do not attempt to leverage the mini-close too early in a demonstration. That *will* feel like a high-pressure sales tactic to your audience and will likely do more damage than good. You almost have to *earn* the right to ask a mini-close question. You need to have reached a point where you have demonstrated a couple of your key points – i.e., you've hit a couple of your *ah-ha moments*. You need to have had some questions from the audience that you were able to answer well. You need to have built some rapport. You need to have effective engagement in the room.

Until you've reached that level of conversation and discussion in the demo, a mini-close is probably premature. But when you do reach that point, do *not* miss the opportunity to go for a mini-close. Strike while the iron is hot.

Remember, our job is to get the technical win. The purpose of the mini-close is to help you get there faster. Below is a list of sample mini-close questions that you can use. Experiment. Not all of them will feel natural to you. Try these and then come up with some of your own.

1. Does it look like this capability will enable you to meet your objectives?
2. Did you see how that capability will satisfy your needs?
3. Will that component comply with your requirements?
4. Are you satisfied with how the tool addressed that requirement?
5. Is there any reason what I just showed you won't give you what you need?
6. Can you imagine using that capability in your environment?
7. Does that align with your current process?
8. Did that address your specific requirements where that was concerned?

The questions are intended to be subtle. They are intended to be used *gently*. And be sure to ask in the context of a small aspect of the software—not the entire thing. You are not asking them if they want to buy the software. You are not asking them if they are completely convinced. You are just asking them if they like one of the things you've shown them. Keep the question very narrow in scope. Keep "mini" in the mini-close. For example, *"Did that one feature that we just covered, does that at least address one of the requirements we talked about?"*

What sort of responses can we expect?

Good question. In fact, critical question. We will typically get one of three responses. And how we handle them is very important.

1. You may get a very positive response. The audience acknowledges that yes, that will meet their needs. If so, great! It means you are well on your way to the technical win. Congratulations! Keep going.

2. You may get a hesitant response, or a partial response. Your audience might come back with, *"Well, we've seen a few things we like, but we're not so sure about..."* And then, more than likely, they'll tell you more about what it is that they are looking for. Perfect! Now we know what we still need to show them to get to the technical win. We know what their concerns are and can steer the conversation in that direction. (By the way, if they don't tell you, ask!)

3. You may get a resistant or a closed response, which might mean the question was a little premature. They might come back with, *"We really haven't seen enough yet to come to any conclusion."* OK. Now we know for sure that the jury is still out. They might even say, *"So far, I'm not sure we've seen quite what we were looking for."* Again, great. Now you have more information to work with. This now becomes an opportunity for you to do some additional discovery. *"Help me understand what it is that you are looking for."* Or *"May I ask what reservations you have so I can better address your concerns?"*

Whatever their response is, you are getting valuable information that you can use to help guide the conversation and steer them towards the technical win.

Habit #5 Action Plan and Take-aways

Understand that a software demonstration is a performance. Know how to engage with your audience. Set boundaries and know the players. Expect and answer questions. When appropriate, pause for effect. Remember to explain but don't over-explain. Know your 'ah-ha' moments and leverage them effectively. Consistently seek feedback. Leverage the "mini-close" to your advantage. Know how to handle setbacks. Do these things and you will dramatically increase your odds for success.

Action plan:
1. Be yourself
2. Establish scope and context up front
3. Know the players
4. Be set up and ready to go
5. Begin with the end
6. Explain but don't over explain
7. Use common terminology
8. Slow down
9. A confused mind always says NO
10. Know and emphasize your aha moments
11. Expect questions
12. Acknowledge the person and the question
13. Assess the person and the question
14. Know how to answer them – The Q&A Quadchart
15. It's OK to say "I don't know"
16. Use the qualified YES
17. Say no without using the word "no"
18. The Power of Saying NO
19. Seek feedback along the way
20. Leverage the mini-close

Learn and apply these tips. Be patient with the process. It will not come overnight. But over time, you will discover that your performances will improve with every demo and the results will speak for themselves.

CHAPTER 8

HABIT #6 - PERFECT

Congratulations! You've made it to the final chapter of the book. If you've come this far, you understand that the first five habits apply to what happens both BEFORE and DURING a sales demonstration. Habit #6 takes place AFTER a sales demonstration. Habit #6 is based on the principle of constant and consistent improvement. Habit #6 is to consistently strive to PERFECT your sales demonstration. That's pronounced "per-FECT", as in the verb not the noun or adjective. Allow me to explain.

No software package, platform, or tool is perfect. They all have their weaknesses, shortcomings and flaws. No demo is going to be perfect. OK, *rarely* is a demo ever going to be perfect. Regardless of how solid the relationship is with your sales counterpart. Regardless of how well you have probed, prepared, and practiced. Regardless of how strong your performance is on stage. Stuff happens. You will be thrown curveballs. Prospects will ask questions you can't answer. They will request things the software cannot do. It will act up in front of the crowd. You will discover data and configurations that weren't set up correctly. Etc. Etc. Etc.

Simply put, stuff happens – no matter to what lengths you go to avoid them. And typically, when you least expect it. The best laid plans, as they say, tend to go awry. As a good friend of mine once said, *"Life is what happens when you've made other plans."* No truer statements can be said of a software demo.

As such, Habit #6 is to consistently strive to perfect the demo. Allow me to qualify what I'm saying here. I am not suggesting that you should work to create the *perfect demo*. It's not realistic, and it's not worth the time investment. Planning for a demo is sort of like training for a marathon. In preparation, runners (I'm told) run, on average, about 5 miles a day for three months leading up to the event. Then, in the weeks leading up to the marathon they take one long run each week, first 10, then 15 and finally 20 miles. But they don't run the full 26 miles until the day of the race. They count on the adrenaline and energy of the day to carry them through that final six miles. (Not that I know this firsthand, by the way, but so I've been told. This is not a book on how to run a marathon, so don't beat me up if I'm off base here.)

The point is that it's not realistic to think that we can create the perfect demo and attempt to prepare, in advance, every single thing we might have to cover. It's impractical to attempt to do so. Like the marathon runner, we should leave the final "6 miles" to the energy and adrenaline of the day.

INSIGHT: One of the complaints I consistently hear from SE managers is around this notion of striving for perfection. They argue that one of their biggest issues is some of their SEs waste time prepping for demos because they are striving for perfection. In their words, "They allow Perfection to become the enemy of Good Enough." Please understand what I'm saying here. I'm not suggesting that you strive for perfection at the expense of good enough. What I'm suggesting is to practice the habit of continual improvement. However, do be careful not to let 'perfection' become the enemy of 'good enough' (or your managers may come after me with shovels and pitch forks).

Think "Pursuit of Mastery"

When I say that Habit #6 is to *perfect* the demo, think the *pursuit of mastery*. In his book *"Drive"*, Daniel Pink sites mastery as one of the three elements of what he calls Motivation 2.0, the theory that intrinsic drives are more powerful than extrinsic drives. He compares mastery to an asymptote. You may have learned the term in algebra. It is "a line that continually approaches a given curve but does not meet it at any finite distance." He references French artist Paul Cézanne, who was known for "endlessly trying to realize his best work," throughout his entire life.

Pink goes on to say that *"Mastery is an asymptote. You can approach it. You can home in on it. You can get really, really, really close to it. But like Cézanne, you can never touch it. Mastery is impossible to fully realize."*

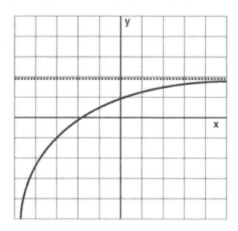

Figure 8: "Mastery is like an asymptote", Daniel Pink

That's how the most effective SEs think of their craft. They are in constant pursuit of mastery, knowing they will never fully get there. There is always something that can be learned, improved, refined. So how do they do this? What do they do that you can learn from and apply to your job?

When something does go wrong, and it typically will. When a question is asked by a prospect for which there isn't a satisfactory answer. When a requirement is discovered that the software doesn't support particularly well. When some portion of the demo underperforms because of a lack of data or a weak configuration. When some part of the message or story or delivery fails to move the customer across the line. The most effective SEs evaluate what went wrong, identify what needs to be changed, and address it before they find themselves in that situation again. They constantly and consistently strive to perfect their game, perfect their demo.

Conversely, if something in a demonstration works particularly well. If some part of the story ends up being the critical moment or a turning point in the conversation, we want to understand and identify that as well. Maybe it was unscripted and just came out "organically". If that's the case, this is something that should possibly be integrated into other demonstrations.

The bottom line is, we need to learn from every demo and apply those lessons to other deals in the pipeline and future deals down the road. So how do we do this?

Before we answer that question, let's consider a more basic question. What are the three typical outcomes of a demonstration, or more broadly, a sales opportunity?

The Three Outcomes of a Sales Opportunity

There are typically three outcomes from any sales opportunity. We either win the deal, we lose the deal, or the deal just sort of drifts aimlessly without any end in sight. Sales meetings that involve a product demonstration tend to follow the same pattern. Either we get the technical win – that's a victory for us. We have a clear fail – "*sorry, not interested*". Or third, we end with a very ambiguous result, whereby the customer seems neither thrilled nor completely turned off. They're sort of tepid on the solution and need more time to consider and discuss.

What can be learned from each of these three scenarios? What can we take away from each of these and apply to other deals in pipeline or future deals?

What can we learn when we win?

When we win, or get the technical win, what was it that seemed to seal the deal? What was it that swayed the customer or prospect in your favor? Was it a key question that was answered? Was it a key capability that you demonstrated? Was it the ability to do something specific with their data or processes? By considering these questions, you may identify new ways to position and talk about your solutions that you hadn't considered before. It may cause you to rethink the way in which you present certain capabilities or the order and flow of your demos. Pay particularly close attention to the unexpected ah-ha moments. Sometimes we take some things in our software for granted that others find unique and exceptional. Learn from those moments and use them to your advantage in the future.

What can we learn when we lose?

Similar to when we win, but in reverse. Were there a series of steps or points that resulted in a logical conclusion or question that you couldn't answer? That is, did you paint yourself into a corner? Did you complete your story to find the customer was expecting more? Look for those aspects of the software itself or your story that turned the meeting for the worse. How can you avoid those in the future? Whenever you lose a deal or fail to get the technical win, there are lessons to be learned. Seek to identify what was missing, where the software fell short, and what might have led to confusion and noise.

What can we learn when there's "no decision"?

If you find that meetings are closing with no clear outcome, no clear decision, we need to attempt to pinpoint the source. Is it related to the software itself? Is it the demonstration – the story, the content, the flow? Is it in our delivery? Are we failing to apply some of the rules from the previous chapter, like seeking feedback or responding to questions appropriately? Ending a meeting with no clear result is almost worse than ending with a loss. (Although the sales folks may not agree with that.) At least with a loss, you know where you stand, and you can assess your mistakes, learn from them and move on. Meetings that end in "no decision" are worse because you don't know exactly where you stand. They may stay on the radar for months, taking up mental bandwidth, and never close. Whenever you have a meeting that ends like this, work hard to identify what can be done to remove some of the uncertainty and ambiguity, and avoid it in future opportunities.

How does this apply to me?

During your demonstrations, pay very close to what works and what doesn't. Observe the audience throughout the meeting. How do they respond to various aspects of the software and story? What questions did they ask and when? Were there questions you couldn't answer? Was it a weakness in the product? Was it a lack of knowledge or familiarity on your part? Did you find yourself painted into a corner as a result of anything you demonstrated? Take notes throughout your demo on things that you need to research, or change, or clean up. If you don't have pen and paper, make mental notes as you go. The answers to all these questions indicate things that you can do to improve the demo before your next customer engagement.

In some cases, there may not have been any negative moments in the demo, per se. There were no questions you couldn't answer, no requirements you couldn't address, etc. But the demo just felt a little flat at times. The story was a bit weak. The data was limited or inconsistent. The message was choppy. There are a range of things that can typically be done to spice up a demo and make it more enticing and engaging. Don't wait until the next demo request to address these items. Before you receive another demo request and find yourself thrust back into the cycle of probe-prepare-practice-perform, take time to do some research. Clean up, fix, or enhance some aspect of the demo under non-urgent conditions. Let's take a page out of Steven Covey's *"The Seven Habits of Highly Effective People."* Be proactive. (Incidentally, clearly his book is better than mine, because he identified seven habits, and I, only six.)

This seems pretty obvious. Why is this even a problem?

We tend to work long hours, for subsequent days leading up to a big demo. In fact, many demos are a "sprint to the finish line". And often, as soon as that demo is over, we are called back to the mat again, with a new opportunity, another set of requirements, another set of objectives, etc. In fact, we can almost become addicted to the adrenaline rush. However, when we do get a break from the melee of requests and inquiries, we often need a day or two to catch our breath. We may not even look at the product, much less think about the demo.

Thus, the *challenge* we have is we often, simply don't have time to address or resolve recurring, long-standing issues, shortcomings and limitations in the software and our story. The *mistake* we make, is that when we *do* have the time, we allow ourselves to become so burned out, that we don't have the energy to address the issues. It becomes a vicious cycle. As a result, we collect "demo debt" along the way. (I'm sure you've heard of *technical debt* before, in the context of software. This is analogous to "demo debt" – stuff that we collect along the way that doesn't show great, but gets the job done, and no one has time to fix.)

To be most effective in our roles – i.e. to achieve the highest level of mastery – we need to reverse this cycle. We need to make time and *take* time, to consistently improve our demos, so that each one is an improvement over the last.

How do we do this?

It begins with asking yourself the questions mentioned above.

- How did the audience respond to various aspects of the software and story?
- What questions did they ask and when?
- Were there questions you couldn't answer?
- Was it a weakness in the product?
- Was it a lack of knowledge or familiarity on your part?
- Did you find yourself painted into a corner as a result of anything you demonstrated?

It also requires the involvement of your sales counterpart – which brings us back to habit #1, the strength of the partnership. After every demo, schedule a debriefing with the sales rep that you partnered with on the demo. Ask him/her for feedback. What did they think worked particularly well? Was there anything they would like to see changed? Were they surprised or disappointed by anything? Was there anything that they were particularly impressed with? Did they see or sense something that maybe you didn't? Also, use this opportunity to provide some feedback to them. Is there anything they could do to better set the stage for the demo?

The Continuous Feedback Loop

Always circle back with your sales counterpart after the demo. Not only are you perfecting the demo, but you're improving the team's overall approach. You're also proactively working on building the relationship. This will pay dividends down the road, in terms of your collective performance together in front of a customer and in terms of your own success. The better relationship you have with your sales teams, the more deals you will be invited into, which gives you the best opportunity to maximize your earnings.

Once you've assessed the demo yourself and received feedback from your sales partner, budget and schedule time to make those enhancements to the demo.

- Look for better ways to answer a certain question
- Build workarounds for requirements the tool doesn't satisfy directly
- Change configurations to give and show a better answer
- Give feedback to the product teams if you discover known limitations
- Research topics you are less knowledgeable on
- Learn or practice elements of the platform you haven't mastered
- Enhance data and views to look more compelling

Over time you will build you own "toolbox" of customizations, configurations, and workarounds for questions the software cannot adequately address on its own. You will collect a set of "canned responses" to the most difficult questions that otherwise throw you off your stride or catch you off guard. You can share these with fellow SEs on your team and in other groups. Collectively you can build a repository of solutions, best practices, etc. You can leverage and share expertise with one another. You can use your knowledge, experience and field solutions to help and train other, more junior SEs. Your workarounds may even drive future development in the products.

One of the most common issues I see in virtually every software company, or with every software package, is there are known weaknesses that never get satisfactorily addressed. The product teams know the weaknesses or shortcomings but don't have the time or money to address all of them. The sales folks nervously talk their way around them. The consultants begrudgingly customize their way through them. Yet, we are the ones that end up holding the bag in front of the customer.

We are the ones put on the spot time and time again, trying to explain away why the tool does this or doesn't do that. Don't let this happen to you. Again, all software packages have their weaknesses. Know what yours are. Discuss them with your sales counterparts. Determine the best way to address them. Build a satisfactory workaround. And avoid finding yourself in that sticky, uncomfortable position.

At the end of the day, it's OK to make a mistake during a demo. It's OK to be unable to answer a question completely or effectively. But if you find a recurring question, or a recurring problem and you don't address it when you have the time, that's not OK.

My first boss in this profession had a system for this. Whenever he gave a demo, if he was asked to show something that he could not or if he was asked if the tool could do something that it could not. The next day, or before the next demo, he would spend time to develop a custom-built solution or workaround. Then, the next time he got that question, he had something prepared that he could show. It may not have been the ideal solution. It may not have been the perfect answer. But at least it was an answer. And after years of doing this, there were very few questions he couldn't address. He never reached perfection. But he also never ceased to strive for it. That's habit #6. To consistently strive to perfect your demo. To consistently strive for mastery. So that over time, you can minimize the number of times you have to say NO. So that you can ultimately convince your audience to say YES – and get the *TECHNICAL WIN*.

• • •

The Six Habits of Highly Effective Sales Engineers

So, there you have it – the Six Habits of Highly Effective Sales Engineers. If you want to become highly successful in this profession; become highly sought after as the expert in the field; paid well – extremely well – for your expertise; admired and welcomed by customers; revered by colleagues; have more time for yourself and your family, and less stress overall in your life, learn, develop, and apply these habits and experience results beyond your wildest expectations.

PARTNER with your sales counterpart. You are in sales, and Sales is a Team Sport.

PROBE into any request for a demonstration. Master the Technical Discovery Call.

PREPARE with the demo in mind. Balance Demo Content with Demo Script.

PRACTICE by Clicking Every Click of significance. Avoid surprises on the other side.

PERFORM when you take the stage. Follow the best practices to get the Technical Win.

PERFECT your demo by applying the principle of Constant and Consistent Improvement.

Do these things and you will become a highly effective, highly satisfied, highly sought after, highly compensated sales engineer.

See the invitation to connect on the next page.

An Invitation to Connect, From Chris...

For starters, if you've gotten this far then allow me to begin by thanking you for purchasing and READING the book. I hope you enjoyed reading it as much as I enjoyed writing it.

Next, I'd like to invite you to connect. Of course, you can find me on LinkedIn, and although you can't click on a link here in the printed copy, I'll include the link to my profile, just in case.

https://www.linkedin.com/in/chris-white-demo-doctor/

I absolutely LOVE to hear from readers, and it would be my distinct privilege and pleasure to make your acquaintance on LinkedIn. I do hope you'll reach out!

I host a weekly LinkedIn Live show on Mondays, now called Tech Sales Advice. Follow the hashtag #techsalesadvice, and you will catch every episode beginning January 2022. Previous episodes can be found on LinkedIn under the #thesixhabitsofhese hashtag.

In addition, if you're at all inspired to do so, I'd like to invite you to consider leaving a review on Amazon. If you like the book and think it might be a worthwhile read for others, please let them know.

And finally, if you found the content useful enough to introduce to your colleagues and/or organization, I have launched and now run a sales training business full time that specializes in training sales engineers and software sales teams – training AEs and SEs together in many cases. We also speak at SKO's and offer a range of enablement solutions – based largely on The Six Habits.

Please visit www.techsalesadvisors.com to learn more.

Thank you! All the best! Chris...   *Chris White*

Another Free Gift...

Want more? Download the *Predictive Model for Demo Success* at
www.demodoctor.com/predictivemodel. **ENJOY!**

Predictive Model for Demo Success

What: The DemoDoctor Predictive Model for Demonstration Success is intended to be a model to determine the probability of success going into any demo and the relative risk factor.

How: Simply review the checklists for each of the Six Habits and give yourself a score in the model for that habit based on the number of items checked. Each habit will receive a score of 0-5.

1. Partner
- I've worked with this AE before.
- We've won deals together before.
- Our styles and approach mesh well.
- I was involved in the sales strategy for this opportunity.
- We agree on the approach for this opportunity.

2. Probe
- I had the opportunity to do technical discovery.
- It was with the right person.
- I asked all the key questions I needed to ask.
- I understand the objectives, requirements and expectations.
- I know who to expect in the demo, who the key players are.

3. Prepare
- I prepared a demo outline for this meeting.
- I have developed a story around the outline.
- I had the time necessary to prepare specific content.
- There is nothing unusual or extraordinary about this demo.
- The demo script is well within the allotted time for the demo.

4. Practice
- I budgeted time to practice the demonstration flow & story.
- I have practiced the demo and "clicked every click".
- The environment I tested is EXACTLY what I will demo.
- Nothing has changed in my environment since I have tested it.
- I gave a walk through for my sales counterpart.

5. Perform
- I know what my 'ah-ha' moments are & why they are important.
- My demo opens with the most enticing, compelling capability.
- I'm prepared to pivot and turn as necessary.
- I'm fully prepared to answer questions & know how to do so.
- I'm fully confident in the demo & the required expertise.

6. Perfect
- My sales counterpart and I debrief regularly after demos.
- There are no outstanding issues from our last customer meeting.
- There are no product limitations that haven't been addressed.
- I'm prepared to address requirements the product can't support.
- I've discussed product concerns I have with my sales counterpart.

Scoring

Score	Interpret as follows
24-30	VERY HIGH probability of success in the demo. Very little risk. On to Victory!
18-23	REASONABLY HIGH probability of success. Potential risk. Proceed but stay on your toes.
12-17	AVERAGE probability of success. Equal part risk. Proceed with caution. Expect the unexpected.
0-11	VERY LOW probability of success. Reconsider the demo. Suggest alternative action, e.g. Discovery.

©DemoDoctor.com   DemoDoctor.com   May 2020

References

"Chapter 1." *Great Demo!: How to Create and Execute Stunning Software Demonstrations*, by Peter E. Cohan, IUniverse, 2005, pp. 1–1.

"Chapter 8." *How to Demonstrate Software So People Buy It*, by Brian Geery, SalesNV, 2016.

"Chapter 5." *Drive: the Surprise Truth about What Motivates Us*, by Daniel H. Pink, Riverhead Books, 2009, pp. 122–124.

Covey, Stephen R. *The 7 Habits of Highly Effective People*. Simon & Schuster, 2005.

Lamson, Marc. "The Go-Around And How We Communicate With Our Customers." *The Go-Around And How We Communicate With Our Customers*, Aslan Training, 20 Oct. 2015, www.aslantraining.com/the-go-around-and-how-we-communicate-with-our-customers/.

Gray, John. Men Are from Mars: Women Are from Venus: A Practical Guide for Improving Communication and Getting What You Want in Your Relationships. HarperCollins Publishers, 1992.

Index

Made in the USA
Las Vegas, NV
05 June 2022

49837732R00108